T0195916

# 40 Days IN THE Wilderness

## A FORTY-DAY DEVOTIONAL FOR CHRISTIANS STRUGGLING WITH DOUBT, DEPRESSION, ANXIETY, ASSURANCE, DISEASE, AND OTHER VARIOUS TRIALS

## KELLY ISAACS

WESTBOW
PRESS®
A DIVISION OF THOMAS NELSON
& ZONDERVAN

WestBow Press books may be ordered through booksellers or by contacting:

WestBow Press
A Division of Thomas Nelson & Zondervan
1663 Liberty Drive
Bloomington, IN 47403
www.westbowpress.com
844-714-3454

ISBN: 979-8-3850-1765-2 (sc)
ISBN: 979-8-3850-1766-9 (hc)
ISBN: 979-8-3850-1767-6 (e)

Library of Congress Control Number: 2024901457

Print information available on the last page.

WestBow Press rev. date: 02/16/2024

# CONTENTS

# INTRODUCTION

Seventeen years ago, when I had my first seizure, I was told that I had to go three months seizure-free before I could drive again. As a young college student, this sounded like the worst news ever! How would I ever make it three months without driving?! Little did I know that this was only the beginning of my journey. I've continued to have seizures until this day. About five years ago, I was diagnosed with major depressive disorder and religious ocd. I experienced terrible, unwanted thoughts. I tried hard to fight them off, but it only felt like a losing battle. I would also obsess over thoughts such as: *what if my faith isn't genuine, what if I've lost my salvation, what if God is punishing me, what if God no longer loves me?* A few years later, my seizures began to increase in frequency. With this came great anxiety. I lived in fear of having a seizure, especially when I was away from home. Satan has tried to use all of these trials to devour me. Many times, I felt as if he had won. I was worn and discouraged. My faith felt weak. I didn't feel God's love or presence. But our God is faithful to us. Even when we feel a million miles away from God, He is working in our lives. His Word tells us that He *never* leaves us or forsakes us. He walks through the fire with us, and in His compassion, He uses our trials for good. His promises to us *never* fail. I can look back, and I can see how much God has grown me. He's used my suffering to help me seek Him more, to humble me, to rely solely on Him, and to teach me. As I sought comfort and answers to my questions, I began writing down any quotes or Bible verses that were helpful to me. Before long, I had an entire journal filled up.

Any time that I felt low or had questions, I would look through that journal to find encouragement. I soon believed that God wanted me to turn that journal into a devotional so that I could share the things that I had learned with others. Jesus said, "In this world you will have trouble. But take heart! I have overcome the world" (John 16:33 NIV). Believers all around the world are suffering, but we can take heart, because Jesus has overcome! We have the great hope of *eternity* with no more pain or sorrow. But until that day, we must cling to Jesus and His promises. My hope and prayer is that this devotional would encourage you and comfort you as you endure the trials of this life.

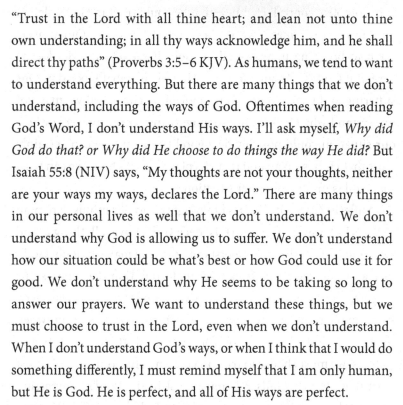

One

# TRUST IN THE LORD

"Trust in the Lord with all thine heart; and lean not unto thine own understanding; in all thy ways acknowledge him, and he shall direct thy paths" (Proverbs 3:5–6 KJV). As humans, we tend to want to understand everything. But there are many things that we don't understand, including the ways of God. Oftentimes when reading God's Word, I don't understand His ways. I'll ask myself, *Why did God do that? or Why did He choose to do things the way He did?* But Isaiah 55:8 (NIV) says, "My thoughts are not your thoughts, neither are your ways my ways, declares the Lord." There are many things in our personal lives as well that we don't understand. We don't understand why God is allowing us to suffer. We don't understand how our situation could be what's best or how God could use it for good. We don't understand why He seems to be taking so long to answer our prayers. We want to understand these things, but we must choose to trust in the Lord, even when we don't understand. When I don't understand God's ways, or when I think that I would do something differently, I must remind myself that I am only human, but He is God. He is perfect, and all of His ways are perfect.

The book of Habakkuk is an excellent example of trusting in the Lord, even when we do not understand. This book shows us God's

1

responses to Habakkuk's questions. Habakkuk didn't understand why his prayers seemed to be going unanswered. Judah had become increasingly wicked, and it seemed as if the Lord hadn't noticed. It seemed as if God was just going to allow them to go unpunished. God may seem silent, but nothing goes unnoticed by God, and He has a plan for everything. God told Habakkuk about His plan, but then Habakkuk didn't understand God's plan. He didn't understand why God would use the Babylonians, a nation even more evil than Judah, to punish them. God told Habakkuk that Babylon would receive its judgment as well in due time. Habakkuk was reminded that God is in complete control. He knew that he could trust in God's plans.

How many times have we been like Habakkuk? Our prayers seem to be going unanswered by God. It seems as if He doesn't care. But God is the same today as He was in Habakkuk's day. Our suffering and trials do not go unnoticed by God. And we may not understand why He is taking so long to answer our prayers or how our situation could possibly be a good thing, but we can certainly trust that He has a plan and that His plan is what's best. We can trust that God is in control of our situation.

Suffering can put all sorts of thoughts into our minds. Jeremiah 17:9 (NIV) says, "The heart is deceitful above all things, and desperately sick; who can understand it?" It can make us doubt God's love and His goodness. It can get us to question if He hears our prayers. It can sometimes even get us to wonder if He is even there. It can make us believe that we are in control of our situation when really it is God who is in control. Despite all these thoughts and feelings, we must choose to trust in God and His promises. We must trust that He *never* fails. We must trust in the Lord's compassion because His compassion can be hard to feel when we suffer. We must trust that He loves us, and He never leaves our side, even when we can't feel a thing. We must trust that He hears all of our cries to Him, even when they seem to be going unanswered.

The passage in Proverbs says, "In *all thy ways* acknowledge Him" (emphasis added). This means that in every situation, whether good or bad, whether we understand or don't understand, we should seek God and trust Him. When Job and his wife had lost nearly everything, his wife told him to curse God. But Job said to his wife, "Shall we accept good from God, and not trouble?" (Job 2:10 NIV). His wife refused to seek God and trust Him when times were hard. But Job, on the other hand, said, "Though he slay me, *yet will I trust in Him*" (Job 13:15 KJV; emphasis added). Because Job continued to trust in the Lord, God blessed him with a double portion of what he originally had. When we are suffering, we must continue to seek God in prayer, and we must choose to trust in Him.

Of course, my mind thinks that being healed is what would be best for me. I wouldn't have to take medication, I wouldn't have to worry about having seizures, and I could just hop in the car anytime I wanted to rather than needing to rely on others for rides. But I must choose to trust that God has a plan for me and that His plan is far greater than mine. I must humbly say, "If this is Your will for me, then Thy will be done." God can see my future, and He's working all things together for my good.

Along with Job, I think of men such as Joseph and David. God allowed them (and many others in the Bible) to go through hardships. It wasn't because God wanted them to suffer. It was because God had a greater plan in mind. He had a reason for their suffering. God turns ugliness into beauty. He takes a situation where we can see nothing good, and He makes something amazing come from it. I'm sure that, just like us, people such as Job, Joseph, and David did not understand why God was allowing hardships in their lives. The Bible even tells us that they had doubts and questions. There were times when they

3

felt abandoned and unloved by God. But they continued to seek Him and trust Him.

The passage in Proverbs also says, "He shall direct thy paths." If we seek God and trust in Him, in the good times *and the bad,* He will surely lead us down the right paths. Just as God used the sufferings of Job, Joseph, and David, we can rest assured that He will use our sufferings for good as well. No matter how bad or how hopeless things may seem from a worldly perspective, we can be sure that God is "working all things together for our good."

If you are suffering and you don't understand why, continue to seek God and put your trust in Him. Remember that your situation does not go unnoticed by God. Trust His promises that He is compassionate, He never leaves you, and He is working all things together for your good. Trust in His perfect timing (which we discuss in a later devotion). Trust that He is the one in control of your situation, and all His ways are good, even if that means allowing you to suffer. Jeremiah 17:7 (NIV) says, "Blessed is the man who trusts in the Lord, whose confidence is in him."

1.  What are some things in your life that make it hard to trust God rather than lean on your own understanding?

2.  Is it hard to trust in God and His plan when you are going through trials/suffering? What can you do to increase your trust in Him?

# Daily Prayer

Father in heaven, thank You for Your Word. Thank You that no matter what our life circumstances may be, we can trust in You. We can trust that You hear every single cry for help, You love us more than we can imagine, and You will take any situation we are going through and use it for our good. Thank You for the many examples You've given us in Your Word showing us how You used suffering and turned it into good. Help us to trust that You are the same today. You have a reason for allowing our suffering, and You will use it for our good. And just as You never abandoned them or stopped loving them during their trials, You never leave us or stop loving us either. Help us, when we are suffering, to seek You, and help us not to trust in what makes sense to us but to trust in You and Your goodness.

# Two

# Wait Patiently For Him

"Be still before the Lord and wait patiently for him" (Psalm 37:7 NIV). Waiting isn't something that most humans enjoy doing. We don't enjoy waiting in lines, waiting for that vacation, or waiting to hear the news from the doctor. We also don't enjoy waiting on God. We want our prayers to be answered *right now*. Waiting on God is difficult, especially when we are suffering. It can feel like God doesn't hear us or like He doesn't care. As I mentioned in the previous devotion, though, our feelings can be deceiving. We must *choose* to believe God's Word over our feelings, and His Word tells us that He *does* hear us and that He *does* care. We must choose to wait patiently for Him as His Word says.

The story of Joseph is one of my favorite stories in the Bible. Joseph is a great example of waiting on the Lord. He was sold into slavery by his brothers. After several years as a slave in Potiphar's house, he was accused of a crime he didn't commit. Things only seemed to be getting worse for Joseph. He was thrown into prison where he spent several years. Joseph spent *thirteen years* waiting on God. I'm sure he had all sorts of thoughts and feelings during that time, just as we do. He may have felt anger, loneliness, and sadness. He may have questioned why God would allow this and why God wasn't delivering him. But no matter how bad things seemed to be, Joseph chose to continue to praise God and trust in Him. And God had a reason for the suffering. After interpreting Pharaoh's dream, Joseph was made second-in-command over all of Egypt, and he saved Egypt and Canaan from the seven-year famine. When Joseph saw his brothers who had sold him into slavery, he said, "You intended to harm me, *but God intended it for good* to accomplish what is now being done, the saving of many lives" (Genesis 50:20 NIV; emphasis added).

Abraham and Sarah are also a great example of waiting patiently. Abraham was promised a son when he was seventy-five years old. I know that if God promised me something, I'd probably be expecting it the next day! But it was *twenty-five years* before Isaac was born! Romans 4:20 (ESV) says, "No unbelief made him [Abraham] waver concerning the promise of God, but he grew strong in his faith as he gave glory to God, fully convinced that God was able to do what he had promised."

Are you going through a trial that feels like it will never end? Does God seem silent? Do things only seem to be getting worse? Remember the stories of Joseph and Abraham and choose to wait patiently for the Lord. God only intends good for us, and He can take any situation and make good come out of it. I'm sure when Joseph was scrubbing floors as a slave, and when he was sitting in that dark dungeon, he could have never imagined what God had in store for him. I'm sure when Abraham was seventy-five years old, he never dreamed that he would not only have a son, but also that the nation of Israel would descend from him.

Charles Spurgeon said, "Wait in prayer. Call on God and spread the case before him. Express your unstaggering confidence in him. Wait in faith, for unfaithful, untrusting waiting is but an insult to the Lord. Believe that if he should keep you waiting even till midnight, yet he will come at the right time. Wait in quiet patience, not murmuring because you are under the affliction, but blessing God for it." Waiting patiently not only means trusting in God's plan and in His timing but also not complaining about your situation or how long it is lasting. It can be hard not to grumble and complain when we are suffering, especially when it has been lingering for several years. Suffering is not fun. But when we remember the truths that God is with us, He loves us, and He has a plan for us, it makes it a lot easier to praise Him rather than complain. It makes the waiting easier.

Don't stop seeking God and trusting in Him. Wait patiently for Him. You don't know what He has planned for you. You don't know how he can take your situation, as hopeless as it might seem, and use it for a greater purpose. Remember God sees your future, and He intends good for you.

1. What's a prayer request that you've been waiting a long time for God to answer?

2. Do you become discouraged or tend to complain in times of waiting? What can you do to help yourself wait patiently on the Lord and trust in Him?

## Daily Prayer

Father in heaven, sometimes it's hard for us to wait, especially when we are suffering. Help us, in the waiting, to remember the stories of Joseph and Abraham. Things may have felt hopeless for both of them. But they continued to trust You in the waiting, and You rewarded their faith. You had great things in store for both of them. And Lord, just as You were always with Joseph and Abraham, help us to trust that You are always with us and that You have a plan for us as well. Help us not to complain, but to trust that You intend to use our situations for our good, and that You love us even if it doesn't feel that way. Help us to wait patiently for You and to trust in Your perfect timing and Your plan.

# *Three*

## *G*OD'S *T*IMING

God's timing. In the previous devotion, I mentioned that most humans do not enjoy waiting, especially when we are suffering, and we are waiting for God to intervene. After seventeen years of praying for healing, I've often asked, "How long oh Lord," as King David asked in Psalm 13. But I know that I must "wait patiently for the Lord" and trust in Him and His timing. God has a reason for everything, *including* the timing of things. I think about the man who was born blind. He had been blind *his entire life.* God could have healed him at any point. But God had a reason for allowing this. It was so that when Jesus walked the earth, He could miraculously heal this man, proving that He was the Messiah and bringing glory to God. His disciples asked why he was born this way. They thought that perhaps it was because of his sins or his parents' sins. Jesus said, "It was not because of his sins or his parents' sins. This happened so the power of God could be seen in him" (John 9:3 NLT).

There was a reason why Joseph was sold into slavery *when* he was and why he got thrown into prison *when* he did. Joseph was in prison at just the right time that the Pharaoh of Egypt needed someone to interpret his dreams. After Joseph interpreted the dreams and gave him advice on what to do, the Pharaoh made Joseph second- in-command. God saw the future. He knew there would be a seven-year famine, and He chose Joseph to be the one who would save the people.

In the story of Lazarus, Martha and Mary sent word to Jesus that Lazarus was ill. But Jesus *intentionally* stayed where He was for two more days before making the trip to their home. "On his arrival, Jesus found that Lazarus had already been in the tomb for four days" (John 11:17 NIV). Why did Jesus wait? Why didn't he immediately go to their home? He didn't even need to go to their home to heal Lazarus. He could have healed him from anywhere. But Jesus knew that many people would be there to comfort Martha and Mary. By raising Lazarus from the dead, Jesus could reveal His glory, and lead many to believe in Him. John 11:45 (NIV) says, "Therefore many of the Jews who had come to visit Mary, and had seen what Jesus did, believed in Him."

As we talked about in the previous devotion, Abraham was promised a son when he was seventy-five years old. But it was *twenty-five years* before Isaac was born! Why so long? I believe it was to demonstrate two things: Abraham's faith and the Lord's faithfulness. Abraham believed that God would fulfill His promise, no matter how long it took or how hopeless it seemed from a human perspective. And God did indeed fulfill His promise. I know that the longer I go without healing, the more tempting it can be to lose hope. But I must trust in God's timing. Even if He chooses not to heal me in this life, I must still choose to trust His plan.

The Israelites were slaves in Egypt for four hundred years! I'm sure that many times they felt like God had abandoned them or forgotten about them, but he did not forget about them. He cared, and He had a plan to deliver them at just the right time. God told Abraham that "for four hundred years your descendants will be

11

strangers in a country not their own" (Genesis 15:14 NIV). I don't know why it was four hundred years, but I do know that God kept his promise; He delivered the Israelites at just the right time. He delivered them when He said He would.

Between the Old Testament and New Testament, there are about four hundred years of silence. I believe perhaps the reason for this was similar to the four hundred years of slavery. When the Israelites were slaves, they were waiting for a "savior" to deliver them from slavery. After four hundred years of slavery, and a time that felt as if God had forgotten about them, He sent Moses to free them. In this time of silence between the Old and New Testament, I'm sure the Israelites felt forgotten once again. But just as God sent Moses to free them from slavery after the long wait, He now sent Jesus, their true Savior, to free them from their sins. Galatians 4:4–5 (NIV; emphasis added) says, "When the *set time* had fully come, God sent His Son, born of a woman, born under law, to redeem those under the law, that we might receive adoption to sonship."

God plans, and His plans *always* come to pass. In Isaiah 37:26 (NIV), He says, "Long ago I ordained it. In days of old I planned it; now I have brought it to pass." He has a plan for each of us as well, and His plan will come to pass *in His perfect timing.* Not only was Jesus born at just the right time, but He will also be returning at just the right time. We've been waiting *2,000 years* for the Lord's return. That seems like a long time to us, but it's only as a couple days with the Lord. Jesus promised to return, and He will fulfill that promise at just the right time.

If you have been going through a long, difficult season, remember that God has not forgotten you or abandoned you. He has a plan. Continue to trust in His plan and His faithfulness. Wait for His perfect timing. It might be longer than you had hoped, but His plans and His timing are always perfect. Remember that what seems like a long time to us isn't necessarily a long time in God's eyes. He always has a reason for the timing of things, even if we do not understand it.

1.  Have you ever felt abandoned by God? If so, was this during a long season of waiting?

2.  Do you believe that God has a plan for you and that His timing is perfect? Does this give you peace?

# Daily Prayer

Father in heaven, thank You that we can trust in Your timing. When it feels like our trials will never end, help us to remember who You are. You're a God who has a plan for Your people, and Your plans *will* come to pass. Help us to trust that Your timing is perfect and that Your plans for us are good. Help us to be like Abraham, who didn't waver in his faith but who rested assured that You would fulfill Your promises, even when things looked hopeless from a worldly perspective. Thank You that You care enough to have good plans for us, even though we don't deserve it.

# *Four*

# *F*AITH OR *F*EELINGS?

Feelings. They can be a wonderful thing. The joy we feel on the holidays. The excitement of bringing home a new baby or going on a trip. The love we feel between our spouse and children. But many times, in our fallen world, we also experience negative feelings. Sadness, fear, anger, etc. And often our feelings can be deceiving. As Christians, we must be discerning. For example, it could be easy for someone who is going through a difficult trial to *feel* like God doesn't love them anymore or to *feel* like He's abandoned them or is angry at them. Believers can also have times when they don't *feel* like doing what is right (praying, reading God's Word, going to church, serving, etc.). We must ask ourselves, "Am I going to believe my feelings, or am I going to choose to believe God's Word, which is true?"

How do we *choose* to believe when our feelings aren't right? We tell ourselves the truth. When I no longer feel loved, I must tell myself that "nothing in all creation will ever be able to separate us from the love of God that is revealed in Christ Jesus our Lord" (Romans 8:39 NLT). When I feel forgotten, I must tell myself that "God has said, 'Never will I leave you; never will I forsake you'" (Hebrews 13:5 NIV). When I feel like God is angry at me, I must tell myself that "there is now no condemnation for those who are in Christ" (Romans

8:1 NIV). Feelings change, and sometimes they are misleading. But God's Word never changes, and it is *always true.* There are many times when I don't feel like doing the right thing. But God has taught me that faith is about the choices that I make, not about the way I feel. When I don't feel like praying or going to church, I choose to do so anyway because I know that it is the right thing to do. I'm not saying that I've never missed a day of prayer or church! But we shouldn't get into the habit of missing these things.

We can see men in the Bible whose feelings weren't so good, but they chose to praise God and trust in His promises, despite what their feelings were telling them. I think Job is the greatest example. He lost nearly everything, including his family, his possessions, and his health. I'm sure that he was feeling miserable! He was probably feeling depressed after losing his family. I'm sure his faith probably felt weak. We read that Job was angry at God and that he had many questions. He *feels* like God is ignoring his cries for help. He *feels* like God doesn't care. He says, "I cry out to you, God, but you do not answer; I stand up, but you merely look at me" (Job 30:20 NIV). I'm sure he probably didn't *feel* like praising God or praying. In fact, he wanted to die. He says, "Why then did you bring me out of the womb? I wish I had died before any eye saw me" (Job 10:18–19 NIV). But regardless of his feelings, he *chose* to continue to trust and praise God. He said, "The Lord gave, and the Lord hath taken away, blessed be the name of the Lord" (Job 1:21 KJV). He also said, "Though He slay me, yet will I trust in Him" (Job 13:15 KJV). Job knew that God is the one true God. He chose to continue to trust in God's goodness and His plan despite the trials that had come upon him. He chose to endure in his faith because he knew that there was nothing greater than our God and that salvation is from Him alone.

Another great example is David. In Psalm 13, he expresses his feelings. He has been pursued by the enemy because Saul was trying to kill him. He's spent much time in hiding. He *feels* like God has forgotten about him. He *feels* sorrow in his heart. He *feels* like the enemy has triumphed over him. But he *chooses* to trust God. He says, "I trust in your unfailing love; my heart rejoices in your salvation" (Psalm 13:5 NIV). He trusts that even though he can't feel God's love, God's love never fails him. And despite the sorrow that he is feeling, he is still able to rejoice because he knows that God is good, and he knows that his salvation is from the Lord.

Joshua, when leading the Israelites, told them to make a *choice* as to whom they would serve. "Choose for yourselves this day whom you will serve ... But as for me and my household, we will serve the Lord" (Joshua 24:15 NIV). I'm sure that many of the Israelites didn't have great feelings. Some may have felt anger toward God for allowing them to wander in the desert for forty years. I'm sure many didn't feel like doing the right thing. But I'm sure that even many of these Israelites who didn't have the right feelings still chose to serve God because they had seen all that He had done. They knew that God had delivered them from slavery, parted the sea, provided them with food and water, and more. They knew that He was the one true God.

How many times have you felt like Job, David, or the Israelites? Maybe you've been crying out to God for healing, but you feel like He's ignoring you or doesn't care. Maybe you feel like your disease, depression, or struggle with sin has triumphed over you. The devil wants us to believe these lies. But we must choose to trust in God, regardless of what our feelings may be telling us. Faith is something that we choose. It isn't always something that we feel. It is often in times of suffering and trials that we don't *feel* our faith, but we *choose* to keep believing because we know that it's the truth. So, when you don't feel like praising, praying, reading the Bible, or going to church...when you feel anger, doubts, forgotten or unloved by God, don't lose heart. Remember that even some of the greatest saints

17

experienced similar feelings. But they *chose* to continue to trust and praise God.

Choose to trust God's Word. We know that His Word is always true—not our feelings. When we struggle with feelings, we can be assured that our faith isn't about the way we are feeling. It is about our choice to believe in Jesus and to believe in His Word. It is about our choice to continue to do the right thing. And remember that even if your feelings aren't good, God still loves you the same. In Psalm 13:5 (ESV; emphasis added) David says, "I have trusted in your *steadfast love.*" Spurgeon said, "There is nothing so deluded as feelings. Christians cannot live by feelings. Let me further tell you that many feelings are the work of Satan, for they are not right feelings. What right have you to set up your feelings against the Word of Christ?"

1. Do you have days when your feelings don't line up with the truth or days when you don't feel like doing the right thing? What is your response?

2. Do you choose to believe God's Word over your feelings? Do you choose to do what's right, even if you don't feel like it?

# Daily Prayer

Father in heaven, thank You that You never change, and Your Word never changes. Thank You that our faith rests in You and what You've done, not in the unstableness of our feelings. Thank You that whether I'm up or down, Your promises remain the same. Lord, help us to be like Job and David. Although they had all sorts of false feelings and probably didn't feel like doing what was right, they chose to trust in Your promises and praise You because You are the one true God, and You are worthy of all our praise. Help us to always choose to believe Your Word, even when our feelings are trying to deceive us. Help us to choose to do the right thing, even though many times we may not feel like it. Help us, on the days that our faith feels weak, to remember that Your love for us remains the same. Thank You that You never leave us or stop loving us.

# Five

# Doubting

Doubting. I've gone through seasons where my faith has felt weak. I've lacked assurance, and I've had many doubts and questions. There have even been times when I've questioned if the Bible was true. These seasons are very difficult for any believer. We want our faith to be strong. We don't want to have any doubts or questions. We want to have full assurance and peace. We want to trust in God's promises. The enemy can use these seasons of doubt to make us feel all kinds of shame, guilt, and fear. He likes to feed our doubts. I could almost hear him whispering in my ear, just as he did with Eve, "Did God *really* say that you're His child? Did God *really* say that you're forgiven? Did God *really* say that no one could snatch you out of His hand? If you were *really* a Christian, you wouldn't have doubts. God must be upset with you for having doubts." And the list could go on.

I started to question if I was truly saved any time I had doubts or a lack of assurance. But while Satan's goal is to get us to hang our heads in despair, Jesus is the lifter of our heads. He not only helps me to overcome my doubts every time, but He's also shown me that occasional doubts and questions don't make me any less of a Christian. As I talked about in the previous devotion, faith is a choice. Faith isn't about never having questions and never having doubts. It's about *choosing* to believe. When I doubt God's Word, I *choose* to say that His Word is true. Satan wants to make me feel alone, like no other believers ever struggle with doubts or questions. But we can find doubt even among many of the believers in God's Word. Most of us know about doubting Thomas who said that he wouldn't believe Jesus had come back to life unless he saw Him and touched Him.

There's John the Baptist, who had faith enough to claim Jesus as the Messiah. When Jesus was walking toward him, he said with confidence, "Look, the Lamb of God, who takes away the sin of the world" (John 1:29 NIV)! But later, as he sat in prison, he began to question if Jesus truly was the Messiah. Trials and suffering can surely lead to doubts and questions. They can lead us to doubt God's love and His goodness. Perhaps, like John, it can even make you question if Jesus truly is the Messiah. Perhaps John believed that Jesus should have been rescuing him from prison rather than allowing him to suffer.

There's also Peter, who had enough faith to step out on the water and walk to Jesus. But when he saw the wind and the waves, he began to doubt. When we take our eyes off Jesus and put them on this world and the trials that we face, it can surely lead to doubt and fear.

King David had many times of doubting and questioning. In the previous devotion, we talked about how he felt as if God had forgotten him. In Psalm 94:19 (NIV), he says "When doubts filled my mind, your comfort gave me renewed hope and cheer." What a comfort to know that even David, who was a man after God's own heart, had doubts. And just as the Lord comforted David and gave him assurance, he does the same for us when we struggle. God will not let His children be led astray. Believers may experience doubts and questions, but their faith will not fail. "He who began a good work in you will carry it on to completion" (Philippians 1:6 NIV).

There's the man who cried, "I believe! Help my unbelief!" (Mark 9:24 ESV). He believed, but he also had doubts and questions. Regardless of the man's doubts and questions, his belief was enough for Christ to heal his son. And the list of people who had doubts could go on.

The beautiful thing about all these stories is that God's grace wins over doubt every time. Doubt didn't take away these believers' salvation. Just acknowledging that our faith is weak and asking God to strengthen it is a sign of faith. I've noticed that in my seasons of doubt, it humbles me more as I admit to God that my faith is weak, and I beg Him to increase it, just as the man who cried, "I believe! Help my unbelief!" God doesn't accept only perfect faith. He is pleased even if we are doubting yet have faith enough to come to Him and ask Him to help us with our doubts. He is pleased even if someone has faith the size of a mustard seed. Matthew 17:20 (NIV) says, "If you have faith as small as a mustard seed, you can say to this mountain, 'move from here to there,' and it will move." I'm sure many of you might be thinking, *If I told a mountain to move, it wouldn't move. Does that mean I have no faith?* We talk more about this in a later devotion called "Those Verses We Question."

Did you know that some of the disciples were doubting, even after seeing the resurrected Jesus? "When they saw him, they worshiped him; but some doubted" (Matthew 28:17 NIV). Jesus knew that some of them were having doubts, but He didn't shame them. He didn't say, "Wait until your faith is perfect and then go and tell the world about me." He told them to go and tell the world about Him *now.* When a believer goes through a season of doubt, they should continue to follow and serve Christ, despite the doubts and questions. And they should acknowledge to God that they are having doubts (He already knows anyway) and ask Him to strengthen their faith. He will surely help you. He will not let you slip out of His hands. He will help you to overcome your doubts, and His grace will have the victory over your doubts every time! Remember that some of the greatest saints struggled with doubts. Remember God's faithfulness to them. He is the same God today. And remember this quote from Spurgeon: "It's not the strength of your faith that saves you, but the strength of him upon whom you rely."

1. Do you ever go through seasons of doubt? Maybe you are like some of these people in the Bible, who one minute have a strong faith, and the next minute have doubts. How do you respond to doubts?

2. Does it bring you comfort to know that even many of the saints in God's Word had doubts?

# Daily Prayer

Father in heaven, I'm so thankful for Your Word, where we can read about believers who experienced the same struggles that believers today experience. I'm so thankful for Your grace. I'm thankful that You don't require perfect faith but only mustard-sized faith. Help us to believe that You don't shame us or leave us when we have doubts. Just as You accepted the man who believed but admitted that he had doubts, You accept us as well. Help us to believe that Your grace has the victory over our doubts. Help us to believe that You will carry us through and that You will help us to overcome our doubts. Please strengthen our faith. Thank You, Lord.

# Six

# Evidence

In the previous devotion, I talked about when the believer has seasons of doubt. I'm sure that every believer, at some point along their Christian journey, has struggled with doubts or weak faith. This often happens during a trial or a difficult season. The pains and sorrows of this life can lead to questions, such as "Is God good? Does God care? or even Does God exist?" Satan likes to use trials to get us to doubt. He hoped to get Job to ask these questions and to turn away from God. But we all know that Job continued to trust God through his sorrows, and this led to blessing.

As I wrote before, we should always choose to believe the truth of God's Word, no matter how bad we feel. When we are going through a season of doubt or weak faith, we should continue to praise Him, seek Him, and spend time in His Word. We desperately need these things in order to strengthen our faith. But there's more that we can do when we are struggling with doubt to help strengthen our faith. We can look all around, and we can see the evidence of God and His goodness. We can see it in our lives, we can see it in His Word, and we can see it in His creation.

I see the evidence in my own life. I see how much He's blessed me. He's given me a wonderful husband, three healthy children, a beautiful home, and the privilege to be able to stay at home with my children. He's given my husband a great job with many benefits. He's allowed us to take many vacations. He's given us more than we need. He has also grown me spiritually. I can see how He's changed me. 2 Corinthians 5:17 (NIV) says, "If anyone is in Christ, the new creation has come. The old has gone, the new is here!" Even though I still mess up a lot, my desire is to do what's right. I desire to please God and to know Him more.

I can see how He's used my trials to draw me closer to Him and to learn more about Him and His Word. I can see how He's protected me. I've had *several* seizures, but they've all been in a safe place, and I haven't acquired any serious injuries. One day, I was home alone and had a seizure. I woke up on the floor, confused and discouraged. I fell asleep and woke up several hours later in my bed. I had no idea how I got there. I concluded that it must have been God who placed me in the bed. I felt His tender love, and it was a reminder that He sees me, and He cares. I can see how God has *always* met our needs. It seems like my husband always gets a raise at just the right time. For example, my children go to a Christian school, so we pay tuition. This year, my youngest is starting school so our tuition rate went up; my husband got a raise just when we needed it. God always provides.

I can also see the evidence for God in His Word. The Old Testament has over three hundred prophecies about Jesus, and He fulfilled *every single one of them!* "The probability that a person could fulfill just eight of these is one in 100,000,000,000,000,000," said Peter Stoner. That is pretty clear and amazing evidence that Jesus is indeed the Messiah. I even see prophecies fulfilled in modern times. The fact that the Israelites were scattered for nearly 2,000 years and then became a nation again in one day is an amazing prophecy fulfillment. "He will gather you again from all the peoples where the Lord your God has scattered you" (Deuteronomy 30:3 ESV). Isaiah

66:8 (ESV) says, "Who has heard such a thing? Who has seen such things? Shall a land be born in one day? Shall a nation be brought forth in one moment?" We know that on May 14, 1948, in one day, Israel became a nation again.

I also see evidence for God in His creation. My son was putting together a solar system model, and it made me think of the wonders of the universe. The fact that we are the perfect distance from the sun and our world spins to give us day and night. Then there's the moon to give us light by night. I think about how *huge* the universe is, including the planets, the galaxies, and the stars. I've always been fascinated with space. There are thought to be over 100 *billion* stars in our galaxy alone! The next closest galaxy to ours is about 2.5 million *light years* away, and we are able to see it with the naked eye! Psalm 19:1 (NIV) says, "The heavens declare the glory of God; the skies proclaim the work of His hands."

Just our tiny little planet alone is filled with beauty and wonders. I look at the mountains, the oceans, the animals, etc. I look at human beings, God's greatest creation, made in His image. Our bodies are extremely complex and amazing. Living with epilepsy, I've learned about the brain. It is said that there are as many neurons in the human brain as there are stars in the Milky Way! These neurons work together as a communication system to send and receive messages from other parts of the body. David said in Psalm 139:14 (NIV), "I praise you because I am fearfully and wonderfully made; your works are wonderful, I know that full well."

Paul tells us that there is clear evidence for God in His creation and that men have no excuse to not believe. Romans 1:20 (NIV) says, "For since the creation of the world God's invisible qualities-His eternal power and divine nature- have been clearly seen, being understood from what has been made, so that people are without excuse." People really are without excuse. God has given us plenty of evidence, and we either choose to believe or we choose not to.

When I'm having doubts, and I ponder on all of this evidence, my doubts are suddenly replaced with praise and awe. Like many of the men in the Bible, I stop dwelling on the present, and I look back at all that God has done. I see how much he's blessed me, I see the fulfillment of His Word, and I see the wonders of His creation. If you are going through a season of doubt, try not to dwell on the doubts and questions. Instead, look at all of the evidence for God and His goodness in your life, in His Word, and in His creation.

1. What things do you see in your life, God's Word, or creation that give you evidence of His existence and His goodness?


2. When you ponder on these things, does it strengthen your faith?

# Daily Prayer

Father in heaven, thank You that You have given us *so much* evidence to prove Your existence and Your goodness! Men really are without excuse when we stop and look around. Lord, when our faith feels weak or we are having doubts, help us to stop and ponder who You are and all that You've done for us. Help us to look at our lives, Your Word, and Your creation. What's most amazing is that You, God Almighty, Creator of all things, care deeply about each and every one of us—enough to take on the form of a humble servant and die for us. And you love us just the same even when we are having doubts. You truly are amazing, and we love You, Lord.

# Seven

## Anxiety

Anxiety is defined as a feeling of fear, dread, and uneasiness. It is the most common mental disorder, affecting nearly 40 million American adults each year. I'll admit, I am one of the 40 million who struggle. After my seizures increased in frequency, I began experiencing anxiety, especially when I left home. Seizures would come upon me so suddenly and unexpectedly so the fear of having a seizure at any place, any time, caused great anxiety. I would sit in the church service and think, *What if I have a seizure right now?* This led to great anxiety. Oftentimes, my husband and I would have to walk out of the service.

To make things worse, my anxiety felt very similar to auras (the feelings I had before seizures). So, when anxiety came upon me, wondering if maybe it was an aura only made the anxiety worse. There were times and places that I would have full-blown anxiety attacks. I never understood the severity or the struggle of anxiety until I started experiencing it myself. But God's Word tells us repeatedly not to fear or be anxious. Did you know that "fear not" appears in the Bible 365 times? One for every day of the year! I don't think that's coincidence. I thought, *OK, God, I want to obey Your Word. I don't want to have this fear and anxiety, but how do I get rid of it?*

God has taught me a lot about my anxiety over the past few years. The anxiety and fear still come, but I must *be intentional* about redirecting my thoughts. The three biggest things that God has taught me regarding fear and anxiety are that 1) He is *always* with me, 2) I must cast my anxiety on Him, and 3) I must trust Him.

Several verses assure us that God is always with us, and because of that, we have no need to fear. The God of the universe is always with us, and He loves us more than we can imagine. Isaiah 41:10 (ESV) says, "Fear not, for I am with you; Be not dismayed, for I am your God." Joshua 1:9 (NIV) is very similar. It says, "Do not be afraid, do not be discouraged, for the Lord your God will be with you wherever you go." Deuteronomy 31:6 (ESV) says, "Be strong and courageous. Do not fear or be in dread of them; for it is the Lord your God who goes with you. He will not leave you or forsake you." Psalm 23:4 (NIV) says, "Even though I walk through the darkest valley, I will fear no evil, for you are with me." Each of these verses reminds us that we have no need to fear because God is with us. He is far more powerful than anything that brings us fear or anxiety.

When anxiety begins to attack me, I redirect my thoughts to the truth that God is right here with me. Sometimes, I picture Him sitting right here next to me, putting His arm around me, and saying, "Don't be afraid, My child. I'm right here." He is my Good Shepherd, and I am His sheep. He takes good care of me, and He never leaves me. When the disciples were on the boat during the storm, they were terrified. But they had no reason to be afraid because Jesus was right there with them. He said to the disciples, "Why are you so afraid? Do you still have no faith" (Mark 4:40 NIV)? He is just as near to us as He was with the disciples on that boat.

Another thing we must be intentional about doing when anxiety attacks is prayer. When anxiety comes, I always say a prayer. Philippians 4:6 (NIV; emphasis added) says, *"Do not be anxious* about anything, but in every situation, *by prayer and petition*, with thanksgiving, present your requests to God." 1 Peter 5:7 (NIV) says, "Cast your anxiety on him, because he cares for you." When anxiety strikes, I tell God that I am afraid. I ask Him to take away the anxiety and to protect me. Philippians 4:6 tells us that we should thank God in our prayers. We should thank God that He hears us, that He is with us, that He cares, and that He is in control. And that leads me to the third thing I do when I am anxious: I choose to trust that God is in control.

I trust that He has heard my prayers, that He cares, and that the situation is in His hands. I trust that whatever happens is what's best. It's a part of God's perfect plan. In Psalm 56:3 (NIV), David said, "When I am afraid, I put my trust in you." Psalm 62:8 (NIV) says, "Trust in Him at all times." So, when you are having anxiety, whatever the cause may be, remember the One who is right there with you, present your fears and anxiety to Him, and then choose to trust that your situation is in His hands.

It can be hard to leave the battle in God's hands. Humans like to be in control. When I have anxiety, I like to try to control it myself (which usually only makes the anxiety worse). I like to try to prevent seizures myself. But I am helpless without God. Only He can take away the anxiety, and only He can prevent seizures. Of course, I don't want a seizure to happen. But when I remember that God is near, when I pray, and then I trust Him, it is much easier to accept the fact that I may have a seizure. It may be out of my control, but I can trust the One who *is* in control. I must humbly say, "Your will be done." That can be hard to say because sometimes the Lord's will includes suffering and trials. But we know that God's will is best and that He has a reason for everything.

I like how David said, "In God I trust. I shall not be afraid. What can flesh do to me" (Psalm 56:4 ESV)? Anxiety and seizures may beat me down. Seizures may injure me, and I've been drained from the battle with anxiety. But they can't prevent God's will from being accomplished in my life. And they can't harm my soul. My soul is eternally secure in the hands of God. This life on earth can be hard. Anxiety is hard. God knows this. Remember that God has a plan for you, and that His plan may involve suffering. When anxiety strikes, be intentional about shifting your focus to the One who is right there next to you, cast your anxiety on Him, and then trust that He is in control of the situation. He loves you, He is good, and whatever happens is a part of His perfect plan.

1. What things, if any, cause you to have anxiety and fear?

2. How do you deal with anxiety? Do you try to control it yourself, or do you cast your anxiety onto God?

# Daily Prayer

Father in heaven, Your Word tells us many times not to fear or be anxious. Yet, many believers still struggle not to be fearful or anxious. When anxiety and fear come upon us, help us to be intentional about shifting our minds to You and Your promises. Help us to remember that You are right here with us. Help us to remember to cast our fear and anxiety on You. Help us to be thankful that You are with us and that You care. And then help us to trust in You. Help us to trust that You are in control, not us. Help us to trust that You understand anxiety, and You care deeply about us. Help us to trust in Your goodness, and to trust that You are working all things together for our good. May this help to give us peace and rest. Thank You, Lord.

# Eight

## JESUS CALMS THE STORM

"And a great windstorm arose, and the waves were breaking into the boat, so that the boat was already filling. But he was in the stern, asleep on the cushion. And they woke him and said to him, 'Teacher, do you not care that we are perishing?' And he awoke and rebuked the wind and said to the sea, 'Peace! Be still!' And the wind ceased, and there was a great calm. He said to them, "Why are you so afraid? Have you still no faith" (Mark 4:37–40 ESV)? There are so many things that Christians can relate to and learn from in this story. Jesus *knew* that the storm was going to come. He could have prevented it, which would have made things a lot easier for the disciples. But just as He allowed this storm, I believe He allows storms in our lives as well. A lot of times when I have seizures, I think, *God, You could have prevented this.* Which is true. But I must believe that He allows them for a reason.

Maybe your storm is anxiety or disease, and you feel terrified like the disciples did. Maybe your storm is the death of a loved one or depression. Maybe your suffering leads you to believe that God doesn't care. Oftentimes, our reactions to storms are natural. But we must choose to turn our attention away from the storm and onto Jesus, even if He seems to be sleeping. The disciples' reaction (fear and wondering if Jesus even cared) was wrong. But the disciples did do one thing right.

They went to Jesus for help. And even with their fear and doubts, Jesus still rebuked the storm. You may recall how in an earlier devotion we talked about how Jesus isn't asking for perfect faith. If we just have mustard-sized faith, faith enough to come to Him and ask Him for help, that's all He requires. After Jesus calmed the storm, He asked the disciples why they were so afraid and where their faith was. Jesus, the Son of God, was right there with them in the boat so they had nothing to fear. They had seen countless miracles, yet they still had doubts.

How many times do we fear a trial that we are going through, even though Jesus is just as close to us as He was to them? And how much evidence of His goodness have we seen, yet we still have doubts? I believe the reason Jesus was asleep and so calm is because He had *perfect* faith. He didn't fear the storm. He knew that the Father was with Him. He knew that He was in control and could do all things. He knew that His time had not yet come so the storm could do him no harm.

This story should be a reminder to us that believers still face many hardships in this life. Jesus knew there would be a storm, yet He still led His disciples right into it. He said, "Let us go over to the other side" (Mark 4:35 NIV). Jesus knows the hardships that we will face, and He could prevent them, but sometimes He leads us right into them. Jesus was right there with the disciples on the boat, but this did not prevent the storm from hitting hard. Just as Jesus is with believers today, we are certainly bound to encounter our own personal storms, and some may be terrifying. As believers though, we know who is in the boat with us. We know that the Son of God is with us and that He never leaves us. We know that He can do all things. We know that whatever happens is a part of His plan. And we know that just as Jesus safely led His disciples to their destination (the other side of the lake), Jesus will be sure that we arrive at our final destination (heaven). Philippians 1:6 (NIV) says, "He who began a good work in you will carry it on to completion."

The disciples were doing everything in their power to save themselves, but they could not. I believe this has spiritual and physical meaning. Man cannot save himself spiritually. Only Jesus can. And many times, man can do nothing to save himself physically (whether it be like the disciples during the storm or a person fighting a disease), but Jesus can. Matthew 19:26 (KJV) says, "With men this is impossible; but with God, all things are possible."

I believe Jesus allowed the storm for a few reasons: 1) to teach the disciples, (2) to bring glory to His name, (3) and to show that God is always with us and will "get us through and to the other side." The disciples learned just how weak their faith was and just how mighty their Savior was. Even though they had seen countless miracles, they *still* had fear and doubts. I believe this humbled them. They realized that their faith was far from perfect, and they realized that they were helpless without Christ. This also brought glory to Jesus. The disciples said, "Who is this? Even the wind and the waves obey him" (Mark 4:41 NIV)! So, if you are in the middle of a storm, remember who is right there with you. There might be nothing that you can do to control it, but trust that Jesus is able. It might seem like He is sleeping or doesn't care, but that is not the case. Pray, and trust that Jesus will carry you through your storm and get you to the other side. Trust that He has a reason for allowing it. This life can be hard. But we have Jesus walking alongside of us.

1. What are some personal storms that you are facing?

2. Are you running to Jesus for help or trying to control it all by yourself? Does it sometimes feel as if He is asleep?

# Daily Prayer

Father in heaven, thank You for putting this story in Your Word and for all the lessons that it teaches to believers today. When we find ourselves in the storms of this life, help us not to be afraid. Help us not to try to control them completely on our own but to run to You for help. Help us to trust that You are always with us. Therefore, we have no reason to fear. Lord, even if it feels like You are asleep, help us to keep running to You for help and to know that You are in complete control. Help us to trust that You will get us through this storm. You will help us to get through this life, and You will be right here with us through it all.

# Nine

## ASSURANCE

Assurance of salvation. It's something that many believers, including myself, have struggled with. I believe we struggle with assurance when we begin to look at ourselves and our feelings rather than Christ and His grace. We may look at ourselves and ask, *Is my faith genuine? Is there evidence in my life that shows I've been saved?"* Or maybe we're struggling with feelings, and this is leading to a lack of assurance. Maybe we don't *feel* God's love or presence. Maybe we don't *feel* joy. These types of questions and feelings can be very distressing to a believer. But I believe the distress we feel can actually be evidence that one is saved. An unbeliever would never struggle with these types of questions.

Every believer wants assurance, and I believe God gives it to us in His Word. Maybe you fear that you can lose your salvation or even that you've already lost it, and this brings a lack of assurance. But God has shown me *many* passages in His Word that teach the doctrine of eternal security. In Ephesians 1:13–14 (NIV; emphasis added), Paul says this to the Ephesian church: "And you also were included in Christ when you heard the message of truth, the gospel of your salvation. When you believed, you were marked in him with a seal, the promised Holy Spirit, who is a deposit *guaranteeing our inheritance* until the redemption of those who are God's possession." A seal showed ownership. The moment we placed our faith in Christ, He gave us the Holy Spirit and said, "I own them now. This is my child." It also says that we are *guaranteed our inheritance* which is freedom from these mortal bodies of sin, and a glorious immortal body which will live with Christ forever. It doesn't say we *might* receive our inheritance as long as we pray every day and never sin. It says we are *guaranteed.*

God owns us now, and He will not allow anything or anyone to steal us from Him. We are His sheep, and He is our Good Shepherd. He takes good care of us. In John 10:28 (ESV; emphasis added), Jesus said, "I give them eternal life, and they will never perish, and *no one* will snatch them out of my hand."

In Philippians 1:6 (NIV; emphasis added), Paul said, "He who began a good work in you *will carry it on to completion* until the day of Christ Jesus." We do not need to fear losing salvation because God's Word tells us that from the moment of our salvation until the day of Christ's return, He will help us to endure. He won't let go of us. It says He *will* carry it on to completion. It doesn't say He *might* carry it on, as long as we're good people and never have doubts or questions.

Romans 8:39 (NIV; emphasis added) says, *"Nothing* will be able to separate us from the love of God in Christ Jesus our Lord." No failures, doubts, depression, or feelings can separate you from God. Have you come to Jesus in repentance and in faith? Jesus said, "All those the Father gives me will come to me, and whoever comes to me *I will never drive away"* (John 6:37 NIV; emphasis added). The Father has given us to Jesus. What an amazing thing to think about. And Jesus promised to *never* drive us away.

Romans 8:30 (NIV; emphasis added) says, "Those He predestined He also called, those He called He also justified, those

He justified He also glorified." When Jesus called us, we came to Him in repentance and in faith. He forgave us our sins and made us righteous by His blood. And this verse *guarantees* that believers will one day be glorified. It doesn't say that believers *might* be glorified as long as they're always filled with joy and as long as they're never anxious. It says they *will* be glorified. What assurance! These are all promises from God and God does not break His promises.

Perhaps you struggle with assurance because you can't remember the time or place where you were saved. I don't remember the time or place, and this used to bother me. John Macarthur said, "I don't know the exact time of my salvation. But I don't judge my salvation by the past. I judge its reality by the present." He also said, "Those today who teach that, the remembrance of a past event, the remembrance of a childhood prayer, the remembrance of a baptism as a legitimate basis for the believer's security and assurance are wrong. The exact time is never the issue. There are some people who don't remember their birth. I don't. My mother told me about it, but I don't remember it. That doesn't mean I'm not alive." If you can't remember the time that you were born again, don't let that bother you. Look at the present. Do you believe in the gospel? Do you have a desire to please God and to know Him more?

Perhaps you struggle with assurance because of the battle with sin in your life. I speak more about this in a later devotion, but as long as we are in these mortal, unglorified bodies, there will be a battle between the flesh and the spirit. The flesh still tempts us, and many times we fail, but the Spirit convicts us of what is right. Do you desire to do what is right even though you fail time and time again? Paul talks about the struggle, but he praises God "who delivers him through Jesus Christ" (Romans 7:25 NIV). Even though we still sin, we've already been delivered from it. There will be a day when we no longer struggle with sin.

Look to Christ and what He's done. Not the things that you are or aren't doing. Any time I struggle with assurance, it's always accompanied by an over evaluation of my thoughts, feelings, and actions. I am *far* from perfect, but praise God, my faith rests not in myself but in Jesus, who *is* perfect. John Bunyan, the author of the famous *Pilgrim's Progress,* struggled with assurance. He wrote, "I saw with the eyes of my soul Jesus Christ at God's right hand; there, I say, was my righteousness; so that wherever I was, or whatever I was doing, God could not say of me, 'He lacks my righteousness,' for that was in front of Him. I also saw that it was not my good frame of heart that made my righteousness better, nor yet my bad frame that made my righteousness worse, for *my righteousness was Jesus Christ* Himself, 'the same yesterday, today, and forever.'"

We must remember that we are not saved because of anything that we do or feel. It is totally because of Christ and what He has done for us. "It is by grace you have been saved, through faith—*and this is not from yourselves*, it is the gift of God" (Ephesians 2:8 NIV; emphasis added). Not only did He save me the moment I believed, but He *keeps* me saved as well. He is constantly interceding for His children, not because we are perfect but because His perfect righteousness has been imputed to us while our sins were laid upon Him. "For our sake he made him to be sin who knew no sin, so that in him we might become the righteousness of God" (2 Corinthians 5:21 ESV). I certainly don't *feel* righteous, but that doesn't take away from the fact that God sees me as righteous because my sins have been forgiven, and I've been clothed in the righteousness of Christ. Amazing grace indeed! Spurgeon said, "Let me beseech thee, look only to Christ; keep thine eyes simply on Him; let His death, His agonies, His groans, His sufferings, His merits, His glories, His intercession, be fresh upon thy mind; when thou wakest in the morning look to Him; when thou liest down at night look to Him."

1. Do you ever lack assurance? If so, does this cause you distress?

2. When do you notice that you tend to lack assurance? Maybe it's when you over evaluate your thoughts, feelings, or actions? Or maybe it's when you are going through a trial?

# Daily Prayer

Father in heaven, thank You so much for Your grace. Thank You that we are saved because of what You did and are doing for us, not because of anything we've done. It's amazing that You loved us enough to pay the price of our sins for us and to clothe us in Your righteousness, even though we don't deserve it at all. Help us, when we struggle with assurance, to take our eyes off ourselves and to trust in You alone for salvation. Salvation is a gift. It's nothing that we've earned. Thank You for Your great promises that assure us that we are saved and that You will keep us saved as well.

# Ten

# THE ACCUSER OF THE BRETHREN

Satan is known as "the accuser of the brethren." He hates God, and he hates God's children. He accused Job of only being a righteous man because he was so prosperous. He said to God, "Stretch out your hand and strike everything he has, and he will surely curse you to your face" (Job 1:11 NIV). He was certain that if Job lost everything, he'd forsake God. This proves that Satan does not know everything. Our God, however, does know everything, and He knew that even if Job lost his family, his possessions, and his health, it would not cause Job to forsake Him. God wouldn't have allowed it if He knew that it would cause Job to turn his back on Him. "No temptation has overtaken you except what is common to humankind. God is faithful; He will not let you be tempted beyond what you can bear. But when you are tempted, he will also provide a way out so that you can endure it" (1 Corinthians 10:13 NIV).

Matthew 24:24 (NIV; emphasis added) says, "For false messiahs and false prophets will appear and perform great signs and wonders to deceive, *if possible*, even the elect." It is not possible for true believers to be overcome by Satan. It can certainly feel that way at times though. Even David said, "How long must I wrestle with my thoughts and day after day have sorrow in my heart? How long will my enemy triumph over me" (Psalm 13:2 NIV)? I have wrestled with unwanted thoughts and doubts for several years, and it can feel as though they have overcome me. It can feel as though I've lost my salvation. This is what Satan wants me to believe. But I know that they will not overcome me. I have overcome because of Christ in me. And God will help me to endure.

God will complete the good work that He started in us. He will help us to endure through every trial. When Job had lost nearly everything, his wife told him to curse God. I'm sure Job was miserable and had a lot of questions. He might have even been tempted to curse God or to turn from Him. But instead, he chose to continue to trust in God. He said, "Though He slay me, yet will I trust in Him" (Job 13:15 KJV). I believe this was the power of the Holy Spirit in him. Romans 8:26 (NIV) says, "The Spirit helps us in our weakness." I can see in my own life how the Spirit has helped me to endure. Battling epilepsy, OCD, depression, anxiety, lack of assurance, and unwanted thoughts for several years, I could just give up or say that God doesn't care. I could be like Job's wife and curse God. This is exactly what Satan wants. But the Spirit helps me to continue to seek God and trust in Him, and I know that God will help me to endure. I know that God will use this situation and turn it into good. Satan wants believers to doubt and to be discouraged. He wants them to stop running to God. He wants us to look at ourselves, our sins, and our struggles. While God, on the other hand, is the lifter of our heads. He wants us to look to Jesus, His love, His grace, and His faithfulness.

You may be going through a difficult trial and perhaps Satan's goal is to get you to stop running to Christ. Perhaps Satan has filled your mind with doubts and lies. Perhaps he has you questioning

God's goodness and His promises. Maybe He is getting you to fear that a sin or a trial is hurting your relationship with Christ. But remember the truth. God's Word is true. God is faithful. He won't give you more than you can handle. God won't let go of you. He will help you to endure, and He will work all things together for your good. Remember that because Job stayed faithful to God, he was blessed with a double portion of what he originally had. When Job was at his worst, completely miserable, he couldn't see what God had in store for him. But he continued to seek and trust God, and God rewarded him.

Maybe you are at your worst. Maybe you feel as if the enemy has triumphed over you. Continue to seek and trust in God. Remember that He is with you in the fire, even if it may not feel that way. He sees your suffering, and He cares. And who knows what He has in store for you or how He will use this trial for your good? When Satan brings suffering and doubts, remember that God is faithful to His children. Satan may try to bring charges against us as he tried to do with Job. He might be telling God to look at our worst sins, and our worst thoughts. But Romans 8:33 (NIV) says, "Who will bring any charge against those whom God has chosen? It is God who justifies."

While Satan is accusing us before God, Jesus is interceding for us. When God looks at us, He sees the righteousness of Christ. And though Satan is roaming about and can still afflict people and cause people to doubt, this will not be forever. During this time, we can trust that God is so much stronger and that God is in control. We can trust that God will not allow Satan to snatch us from His hands. We can trust that God will walk us through the fire and help us to endure. Satan's time of roaming free is quickly coming to an end. We have this great promise to look forward to: "Now have come the salvation and the power and the kingdom of our God, and the authority of His Messiah. For the accuser of our brothers and sisters, who accuses them before our God day and night, has been hurled down. They triumphed over him by the blood of the Lamb and by the word of their testimony" (Revelation 12:10–11 NIV).

1. Do you ever feel like Satan is attacking you? How so? Have you ever felt like he has triumphed over you?

2. Have you seen how the Holy Spirit helps you in your weakness? In what way? Maybe He's helped you to resist temptation. Maybe He's helped you stay faithful to God through a long, difficult trial.

# Daily Prayer

Father in heaven, I'm so thankful that You defeated Satan at the cross. He may still accuse us and try to tear us down, but You, Lord, are interceding for us. Help us not to believe in Satan's lies but help us to always believe the truth of Your Word. Help us to be like Job. When we are going through difficult trials, even if we are miserable, I pray that we will continue to trust in You. Help us to know that You are walking through the fire with us, and You will help us to endure. Help us to trust that You will use our situations for good. Thank You that Satan cannot steal our salvation. He can steal our health, wealth, etc., but our souls are eternally secure in Your hands. And thank You that one day, Satan will be hurled down and no longer able to accuse us or bring us pain.

# Eleven

# God Allows Trials

Many churches today preach a prosperity gospel: That if we just have enough faith, or give enough, or even do enough good deeds, then we won't suffer. God will bless us with wealth and health. Of course, faith, giving, and good deeds are all good things. Things that believers should practice. But this does not mean that life will be a smooth, easy ride. In fact, the Bible teaches us that God *does* allow trials and that we *will* have trouble in this world. In Psalm 71:20 (NLT; emphasis added), David says, "You have *allowed* me to suffer much hardship." And in John 16:33 (NIV; emphasis added), Jesus says, "In this world you *will* have trouble." Let's look at some examples in the Bible of where God allowed trial and trouble to come upon believers. Truthfully, there are so many examples. I can't think of many believers who *didn't* undergo suffering, but we'll take a look at a few of them. God doesn't allow trials for no reason or because He is harsh. His Word tells us that He is full of compassion. As you will see, God had a reason for the suffering.

God allowed Joseph to be sold into slavery and then be put in prison for a crime that he didn't commit. This suffering led to Joseph becoming a ruler of Egypt and saving the land and his family from famine. David, who was a man after God's own heart, suffered many things. David spent much of his time fleeing and hiding from Saul, who was trying to kill him. I believe there were many purposes for this. David was a "type of Christ," meaning that much of his life pointed to Jesus. David was a shepherd boy and he was Israel's great king, just as Christ is our Great Shepherd and He is our everlasting King. But David was rejected by Saul, just as Jesus was rejected by the people. David suffered much, just as Jesus did. Another reason why God may have allowed David's trials is because during his time of hiding, David was able to write many of the psalms that we read today.

Then there's Job, who was a righteous man, but God allowed Satan to take his wealth, his family, and his health. Job's three friends tried to tell Job that God would never allow a righteous to man suffer (just like many prosperity preachers do today). They told Job that he must have done something wrong, and that God was punishing him. God's response was "I am angry with you (Eliphaz) and your two friends, because you have not spoken the truth about me" (Job 42:7 NIV). So as a side note, we should never assume that our trials and suffering are a sign that God is punishing us. Job stayed faithful to God through the suffering, and God blessed Job with a double portion of what He originally had. I believe this happened to teach believers many things, including the following: we are not exempt from suffering, suffering is not a punishment or a lack of righteousness, we should stay faithful to God in the trials, and God blesses those who stay faithful to Him, whether it be in this lifetime, or in eternity.

In the New Testament, I think about the blind man who Jesus healed. He had been blind his entire life. God could have prevented this or healed him right at birth. Why did God allow this? Jesus said, "this happened so that the works of God might be displayed in him" (John 9:3). We also see Jesus suffering. If anyone deserved *not* to suffer, it was Jesus, yet He was known as "the Suffering Servant" (Isaiah 53). Jesus suffered more than any of the other examples, but His suffering led to salvation and everlasting life to anyone who believes in Him.

Another example in the New Testament is Paul. We read about Paul being tortured by the Jews several times, being in danger, going without food and water, and more. This showed Paul's perseverance and reliance on God, which we talk about in later devotions. Paul also said "that a thorn was given me in the flesh, a messenger of Satan to harass me" (2 Corinthians 12:7 ESV). If we continue reading, we find out *why* the thorn was given. Paul says it was "to keep me from becoming conceited" (2 Corinthians 12:7 ESV).

God allowed Paul, along with all but one of the other apostles, to be persecuted and even martyred for their faith. 2 Timothy 3:12 (NIV) says, "Everyone who wants to live a godly life in Christ Jesus will be persecuted." Christians all around the world are being persecuted. Christians in America have it easier than most other nations, but even here in America, Christians are laughed at, mocked, and hated for their faith. Some have even lost their businesses or been arrested for standing up for what's right. But just imagine their reward in heaven! Jesus said, "Blessed are you when people insult you, persecute you and falsely say all kinds of evil against you because of me. Rejoice and be glad, because great is your reward in heaven" (Matthew 5:12 NIV).

John was the only apostle who was not martyred, but he still suffered. He was exiled to the island of Patmos. And I believe the reason for this was so that he could write the book of Revelation, which tells us about the end times and eternity.

Knowing that God does allow trials and that we will face troubles in this world can be a great comfort to believers, especially when we live in a day where we are told by many that Christians shouldn't suffer. I know that for many years I struggled because I thought that perhaps I just wasn't "a good enough" Christian. Knowing that God uses the suffering for good is an even greater comfort. I can be assured that God has a reason for saying no to my requests for healing, and I can be assured that His plans for me are good.

Stay faithful to God in your suffering and remember that He has good things in store for you. Remember that He is "the Father of compassion" (2 Corinthians 1:3 NIV). Even though you may not feel His compassion, He cares about you more than anyone. Perhaps that is why He is allowing your trial. Because He knows the good that will come from it. God did not promise us an easy life, but He did promise that "He causes everything to work together for the good of those who love Him" (Romans 8:28 NLT).

1. Do you believe that God allows believers to suffer? Why or why not?

2. Can you look back to a past trial in your life (or in someone else's life) and see how God used it for good?

# $\mathcal{D}$aily $\mathcal{P}$rayer

Father in heaven, Your Word teaches us that You do allow suffering and that in this world we will have trouble. But You also promise to work all things together for the good of those who love You. Just as You used the suffering of the believers in Your Word and turned it into good, we can trust that You will use our suffering for good as well. Lord, we know that You are able to do all things. Many of us are suffering, and we know that You are able to take the suffering away. If You choose not to, help us to trust that You have a plan. Help us to stay faithful to You through the suffering. And Lord, even though this life can be hard, help us to always remember that we have an eternity waiting for us where there will be no more pain or sorrow. If it weren't for Jesus and the suffering that He endured, then we would not have that hope. Thank You, Jesus!

# Twelve

## REASONS FOR OUR SUFFERINGS

In the previous devotion, we talked about the fact that believers are not exempt from suffering and hardships. We talked about some of the believers in the Bible who suffered. We also talked about the fact that God has a reason for the suffering, and how He works all things together for good. We saw that God used the suffering of believers in the Bible and made something good come from it. Today, I want to talk about a few reasons why I believe God allows suffering in a believer's life. We've seen what God did through the suffering of Joseph. God might have a plan for us that we could never imagine. But there are several other reasons why I believe God allows trials.

One of the reasons is to help us rely more on God than ourselves. In Paul's letter to the Corinthians, he tells them of the hardships that he faced while in the province of Asia. He also told them the *reason why* he faced hardships. "This happened that we might not rely on ourselves but on God, who raises the dead" (2 Corinthians 1:9 NIV). Are you going through a trial that is out of your control? Maybe it's the loss of a loved one or a chronic disease. There's nothing that *you* can do to improve the situation. It's in times like these that we seek God more and rely solely on him for comfort and healing.

Another reason why God allows suffering is so that we can learn his decrees. Psalm 119:71 (NIV) says, "It was good for me to be afflicted, so that I might learn Your decrees." Before my hardships, I was a believer, but I didn't really dig deep into God's Word and do a lot of studying. Over the past few years, I have learned so much more about God and His Word as I seek answers and seek to know Him more.

In Deuteronomy 8:3 (ESV; emphasis added), we see the hardships of the Israelites. God "humbled them and *let them hunger.*" God said, "Man does not live by bread alone, but man lives by every word that comes from the mouth of the Lord." I believe that God was allowing their hunger for a couple of reasons. One reason was to humble them. If they just had all the food they wanted, whenever they wanted, then they wouldn't need to turn to God and rely on Him for food. And God did provide them with manna when Moses sought God for help. Also, I believe God was telling them that feeding on the Word is more important. The Word of God nourishes our faith and our spiritual growth. While we do need food, we need Jesus a lot more. Perhaps the Israelites only cared about physical needs such as food, but God wanted them to realize how much they needed him. They needed Him to save them not only physically, but also spiritually.

Another reason why God allows suffering is so that we have the opportunity to persevere and become stronger believers. James 1:3–4 (NIV) says, "The testing of your faith produces perseverance. Let perseverance finish its work so that you may be mature and complete, not lacking anything." The testing of our faith can be anything that tries to destroy our faith, such as sickness, the loss of a loved one, depression, and spiritual battles. These things give us the opportunity to persevere, to continue to trust in God and choose to do what is right through the hardships. This leads to a more "mature and complete" believer. And as I've mentioned, God will surely give believers the strength we need to persevere. As we saw in the previous devotion, many believers went through trials, but they all persevered. And God blessed them, which is another reason why I believe God allows suffering in believers' lives.

God desires to bless us because He loves us, and we are His children. If we stay faithful to God through trials, He will surely bless us, whether it be earthly blessings or heavenly blessings. "Blessed is the one who perseveres under trial because, having stood the test, that person will receive the crown of life that the Lord has promised to those who love him" (James 1:12 NIV).

God also allows trials so that people have the chance to prove the genuineness of their faith. "These trials will show that your faith is genuine. It is being tested as fire tests and purifies gold-though your faith is far more precious than mere gold. So when your faith remains strong through many trials, it will bring you much praise and glory and honor on the day when Jesus Christ is revealed to the whole world" (1 Peter 1:7 NLT). Many people might say that they have faith, but their faith is not genuine. I think of Job's wife. After all of the hardships, she told Job to curse God. Job said, "You are talking like a foolish woman. Shall we accept good from God, and not trouble?" (Job 2:10 NIV). Those who claim to have faith but then lose their faith or turn from God when hardships come never had genuine faith to begin with. "They went out from us, but they did not really belong to us. For if they had belonged to us, they would have remained with us" (1 John 2:19 NIV). But those who, like Job, continue to trust in God through the hardships will show the genuineness of their faith, and this will be rewarded.

2 Corinthians 4:17 (NIV) says, "Our light and momentary troubles are achieving for us an eternal glory that far outweighs them all." I love this verse because it's a reminder that no matter what we are going through on earth, no matter how difficult or heavy our burdens are, they are only temporary, and they can't even begin

to compare with the "heaviness" of glory that we will have for all eternity. Psalm 34:19 (NIV) says, "The righteous person may have many troubles, but the Lord delivers him from them all." This is just another verse that shows us that we as believers are not exempt from troubles. But we can always have hope. The Lord may decide to deliver us in this life, but if not, we know that in heaven, we will be delivered from sickness, sadness, evil, etc. for *all of* eternity! Continue to trust God through your hardships and keep your eyes on Him and on the glory that awaits us!

1. Does it bring you comfort to know that God has reasons for allowing trials?

2. Is it difficult, the longer you suffer, to continue to trust that God has a reason? Do you sometimes feel forgotten or unheard?

# Daily Prayer

Father in heaven, thank You that we can trust You in our suffering. We can trust that You have a reason for allowing us to go through it. Whether it be to help us rely more on You, to help us seek You more, to humble us, to give us the opportunity to persevere, or to do something in our lives that we never imagined... we know that You will use our suffering for our good. Thank You that You care enough about us to do what's best for us. Lord, we may not understand why You are allowing the suffering, and we may feel forgotten in these times, but help us to remember that You never abandon us and that You are full of compassion. Please give us peace in the suffering knowing that You care about us and what's best for us.

# Thirteen

## God's Love

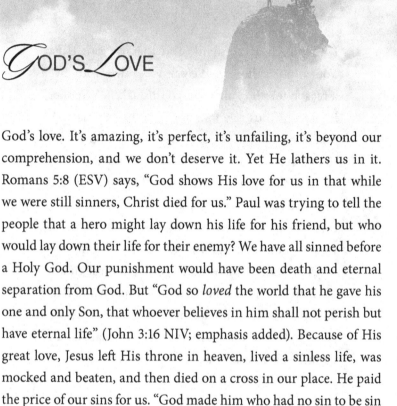

God's love. It's amazing, it's perfect, it's unfailing, it's beyond our comprehension, and we don't deserve it. Yet He lathers us in it. Romans 5:8 (ESV) says, "God shows His love for us in that while we were still sinners, Christ died for us." Paul was trying to tell the people that a hero might lay down his life for his friend, but who would lay down their life for their enemy? We have all sinned before a Holy God. Our punishment would have been death and eternal separation from God. But "God so *loved* the world that he gave his one and only Son, that whoever believes in him shall not perish but have eternal life" (John 3:16 NIV; emphasis added). Because of His great love, Jesus left His throne in heaven, lived a sinless life, was mocked and beaten, and then died on a cross in our place. He paid the price of our sins for us. "God made him who had no sin to be sin for us, so that in him we might become the righteousness of God" (2 Corinthians 5:21 NIV). Paul said that we were helpless to save ourselves, so Jesus did what needed to be done. He lived a sinless life, took our sins upon himself, and imputed His righteousness to us. Not only did God send His Son to save us, but He even sees us as righteous now, and He calls us His beloved children! "See what kind of love the Father has given to us, that we should be called children of God, and so we are" (1 John 3:1 ESV)!

God's love is also unfailing. There are many verses in the Bible that speak of His unfailing love, but I think my favorite is Isaiah 54:10 (NIV; emphasis added). "Though the mountains be shaken and the hills be removed, yet my *unfailing love* for you will not be shaken." I also love Romans 8:35-37 (NLT), which says, "Does it mean he no longer loves us if we have trouble, or calamity, or are persecuted, or hungry, or destitute, or in danger, or threatened with death? No, despite all these things, overwhelming victory is ours through Christ, who loved us." Both of these passages have the same message. These passages teach us that God will *never* stop loving us, no matter what. He doesn't stop loving me if I mess up or if my faith feels weak. No matter what I'm feeling, no matter what my circumstances, whether I'm up or down, God will never stop loving me.

And His love is unchanging. He doesn't love me more one day and less the other. He doesn't love me more when I'm doing good deeds, and less when I'm struggling. He loves me just the same even when I mess up and have bad days. We may not feel His love, but it never leaves us. Maybe you are struggling with sin, or you are going through a difficult trial, and you wonder if He still loves you. Romans 8:39 (NLT; emphasis added) says that "NOTHING in all creation will ever be able to separate us from the love of God." When King David committed adultery and murder, he may have wondered if God still loved him. While there were consequences for his sins, God's love for him didn't change. I'm sure Joseph and Job and many others didn't *feel* God's love in their suffering. But God's love for them hadn't changed.

God shows His love to us in many ways. It's seen most clearly in Christ's sacrifice, but it's also seen all throughout the Bible. The word *love* appears 551 times in the New International Version. In the Old

Testament, we see God's love in how He took care of His people and was faithful to them. He delivered the Israelites from slavery and led them to the Promised Land. He made a way through the Red Sea. He provided food and water. Even when the Israelites sinned, God still loved them and took care of them and was faithful to them. Just as with David, there were consequences for their sins, but God still loved them the same. "The Lord is compassionate and gracious, slow to anger, abounding in love" (Psalm 103:8 NIV). The Israelites messed up time and time again, just as we do, but God was faithful to them, and He continued to love them.

In the New Testament, we can clearly see the love of God through His Son, Jesus. He healed the sick, fed the hungry, and preached the good news. He was full of compassion, just as we read in Psalm 103:8. In Matthew 14:14 (ESV; emphasis added) we read, "When he went ashore he saw a great crowd, and *he had compassion on them* and healed their sick."

We can be assured that the God of the Bible is the same today. I believe the story of the Israelites in the Old Testament is a picture of the church. God loved them, he took care of their needs, he was faithful to them, and he brought them to the Promised Land, even though they didn't deserve it. And just as He was full of compassion in the Bible, He is still full of compassion today. You may not feel His love but remind yourself of what Christ did for you. Remember that because of His sacrifice, God calls you His child and has given you eternal life. Remember that this life can be filled with troubles, but eternal life will be without sorrow.

It's amazing to think that the God of all the universe loved us enough to die for us so that we could be made righteous in His sight. Colossians 1:22 (NIV) says, "But now he has reconciled you by Christ's physical body through death to present you holy in his sight, without blemish and free from accusation." It's amazing that He is faithful to us and cares about everything that we are going through, and that He will use whatever we are going through for our good. It's amazing to think that His love for us never changes, even though we mess up time and time again. God's love truly is amazing.

1.  Do you sometimes forget about how great God's love is? What are some of your favorite passages about God's love?

2.  Do you sometimes struggle to feel God's love or even wonder if He does love you at all? If so, what are some passages/promises from God's Word that can help you to know that you are loved?

# Daily Prayer

Father in heaven, thank You so much for Your great love. Lord, sometimes we forget just how great Your love is. We sinned against You, and we deserve death, but Lord, You loved us so much that You gave Your Son, Jesus, to die for us and take our sins upon Himself. Not only do we now have eternal life, but You have clothed us in Your righteousness, and You call us Your beloved children! Lord, help us, when we struggle to feel Your love, to know that it's always there. Your love for us never changes. Also, there is nothing that can separate us from Your love. Help us when we are suffering, to know that You are full of compassion. Lord, Your love is greater than we can imagine, and we don't deserve it. Thank You for Your love.

# Fourteen

# God's Power

"I am the Lord, the God of all mankind. Is anything too hard for me?" (Jeremiah 32:27 NIV). When this was written, Israel had once again turned to idolatry and refused to obey God, and because of this, they would be taken captive by the Babylonians for seventy years. But God reassured Jeremiah that He would deliver them. After the seventy years, God kept His promise and delivered them from the hands of the Babylonians. Nothing is too hard for Him. He was greater and more powerful than the Babylonians. He is greater and more powerful than anything. Whatever He says goes. Sometimes literally.

Think about creation. "The Lord merely spoke, and the heavens were created. He breathed the word, and all the stars were born" (Psalm 33:6 NLT). He told the plants, animals, oceans, mountains, and stars to appear, and they appeared. Jesus spoke to the wind and the waves, and they obeyed Him. Jesus said to a dead man, "Lazarus, come out! And the dead man came out" (John 11:43–44 NLT).

He "formed a man from the dust of the ground and breathed into his nostrils the breath of life, and the man became a living being" (Genesis 2:7 NIV). He parted the sea for the Israelites. He rained down manna from heaven and made water flow from a rock. He shut the mouths of lions. He shielded the fire from Shadrach, Meshach, and Abednego. Jesus healed many who were sick, opened the eyes of the blind, walked on water, fed multitudes, and brought the dead to life. There is *nothing* that our God can't do.

I love the story about the woman who was healed of her bleeding condition. "A woman had suffered for twelve years with constant bleeding. She had suffered a great deal from many doctors, and over the years she had spent everything she had to pay them, but she had gotten no better. In fact, she had gotten worse" (Mark 5:25–26 NLT). Things seemed hopeless for her. There was nothing anyone could do to help her. But Jesus was able. "She touched His robe ... and immediately the bleeding stopped, and she could feel in her body that she had been healed of her terrible condition" (Mark 5:27–29 NLT). Verse 30 says, "Jesus realized at once that healing power had gone out from him." This shows us just how powerful our God is. The woman simply touched the robe of Jesus, and she was healed.

This passage can be such an encouragement to anyone who has been suffering for a long time and has tried all they could, but everything has failed them. I know that for me, this passage is very dear to my heart. I've had epilepsy for seventeen years. I've been to several doctors, even the best of the best, but they've all been unable to help me. In fact, my condition has only grown worse, just as it did with the woman who had bleeding. Things may seem hopeless from a human perspective, but as believers, we are never without hope.

If I weren't a believer, I would be hopeless. I would fall into despair. But I know who my God is, and I know how mighty He is. When the doctors tell me there's nothing they can do, I know that God is able. I know that nothing is too hard for Him. So, I continue to ask Him for healing, knowing that He is able. As we've talked about in previous devotions, I know that I need to wait patiently for Him. I need to wait for His perfect timing. I need to be persistent. I also know that God allows trials, but He uses them for good. I know that God sees me, hears me, and is full of compassion. I know that whatever happens, I can trust in Him.

I believe God allowed this woman to have her condition for so long and allowed it to get worse so that He could reveal His mighty power and so that many would come to believe in Him. It also points us to the gospel. Jesus said to the woman, "Daughter, your faith has made you well. Go in peace. Your suffering is over" (Mark 5:34 NLT). Realize that He called her "daughter" because of her faith. Jesus calls us His children as well if we've simply believed in Him and come to Him in repentance.

We've talked about how God promised Abraham and Sarah a son. To the world, this seemed impossible because Abraham and Sarah were very old. Even Sarah laughed and doubted. But God said, *"Is anything too hard for the Lord?"* (Genesis 18:14 ESV; emphasis added). God kept His promise, and Abraham and Sarah did indeed have a son. What I love about this is that it was *twenty-five years* after the promise that God would give them a son. To the world, the passing time would have made it seem more and more unlikely that Sarah would ever have a child. Just as it is today, if someone suffers with a disease, the longer they go without seeing results, the more unlikely it seems that they will ever be cured. The story of Abraham and Sarah, and the story of the woman with the issue of blood, both reveal God's mighty power.

If you've gone a long time without healing and you've done all that you could, don't lose hope. If things are only getting worse for you, continue to trust in God. Remind yourself of the woman who had constant bleeding for twelve years. Remember, God could have prevented her from having this condition. He could have healed her sooner. But He has a reason for everything. His healing of this woman revealed His mighty power and led many to believe in Him.

Trust in His power and trust in His plan. Charles Spurgeon said this: "However great my troubles are, they are not as great as my Father's power. However difficult my circumstances may be, yet all things around me are working for good."

1. Have you been going through a long trial? Have things only been getting worse? Has this caused you to lose hope, or do you continue to trust in Jesus?

2. Do you tend to put your hope more in doctors and medicine or in Jesus?

# Daily Prayer

Father in heaven, we know that *nothing* is impossible for You. You are mighty and powerful yet full of compassion. You are an awesome God and the one true God. Lord, help us not to put our hope in doctors and medicine but to put our hope in You. Doctors and medicines can fail us. Help this not to discourage believers. Instead, help them to remember that nothing is impossible with You. Help us to be persistent in seeking You for healing, no matter how long it may take. Help us to trust in Your perfect timing and help us to trust that You hear our prayers, and You care about each one of us. Help us to trust in Your plan.

# Fifteen

# The Lord Is My Shepherd

How comforting it is to know that "the Lord is my shepherd." We are His sheep, and He is our shepherd. Did you ever wonder why God chose sheep as the animal to compare us to? One reason why God compares us to sheep is because they recognize their shepherd's voice, and they will flee from a stranger's voice. Sheep are very loyal to their shepherd, and a good shepherd is very loyal to them as well. Christians recognize that Jesus is the one true Messiah. We follow Him alone and have a relationship with Him. We flee from any false teacher or any false gospel that is preached. Jesus said, "I am the good shepherd; *I know my sheep and my sheep know me,* and I lay down my life for the sheep" (John 10:14–15 NIV; emphasis added). He also said, *"My sheep listen to my voice; I know them and they follow me. I give them eternal life, and they shall never perish; and no one will snatch them out of my hand"* (John 10:27–28 NIV; emphasis added).

Another reason we are like sheep is because just as sheep are prone to wandering away from the flock, so too can Christians get off-track and wander away from the church and from what is true. Jesus said, "What do you think? If a man owns a hundred sheep, and one of them wanders away, will he not leave the ninety-nine on the hills and go to look for the one that wandered off? And if he finds it, truly I tell you, he is happier about that one sheep than about the ninety-nine that did not wander off. In the same way your Father in heaven is not willing that any of these little ones should perish" (Matthew 18:12–14 NIV). As we talked about in a previous devotion, God will not allow any of His children to be snatched out of His hand. I know that during my college years, I wandered from the truth. I began hanging out with the wrong crowd and started doing the things that they did. I didn't have much of a relationship with God. But I'm so thankful that the Lord found me, His lost sheep, and brought me back to where I belong.

Another reason we are compared to sheep is because they do not have to carry heavy loads on their backs like other animals do, and Christians are not meant to carry heavy loads either. Christ has not only freed us from the bondage of sin, but we are to "cast our cares onto him" (Psalm 55:22 NIV). And while most religions are a burdensome work-based religion, Christianity is about grace. It's about what our Good Shepherd did for us, laying down his life. It's not about what we've done.

Sheep are also unable to find new pastures or water without their shepherd. They need the shepherd to lead them and to guide them to food and water, just as we need Jesus to lead and guide in our lives. He helps to give us wisdom and discernment to make the right choices. Psalm 23:3 (ESV) says, "He leads me in paths of righteousness for his name's sake." And just as a good shepherd makes his sheep content, Jesus also gives us contentment. He is all that we need. "The Lord is my shepherd. *I lack nothing.* He makes me lie down in green pastures, he leads me beside quiet waters" (Psalm 23:1–2 NIV; emphasis added). Even if believers are going through hard times, we can still have joy and contentment knowing that Jesus

71

is our Lord and Savior. And we have the hope of spending eternity with Him.

Sheep are defenseless as well. There's nothing they can do to save themselves from the enemy, making them very prone to attacks. They need their shepherd. Psalm 23:4 (NIV) says, "Even though I walk through the darkest valley, I will fear no evil, for you are with me; your rod and your staff, they comfort me." The shepherd's rod was often used as a weapon to fight off wild animals. Christ, our Good Shepherd, has saved us from the enemy of sin. And though the enemy still roams free, and we continue to go through hardships, Christ continues to protect us. When we sin, He is in heaven interceding for us. When the enemy tries to destroy us, Christ fights the battles for us, and He protects us.

We can rest in the arms of our Good Shepherd knowing that He is in control, He cares about us, and no one can snatch us from His hands. There is no greater shepherd. We really are a lot like sheep, and Jesus is indeed our Good Shepherd. We have a relationship with Him, He cares for us, He leads us and guides us, He provides for us, He protects us, and He saves us from the enemy. If you are going through a trial, remember that the Lord is your shepherd, and He is always with you.

1. Have you ever "wandered away from the flock?" Did God find you and bring you back?

2. Does it bring you comfort to know that you are like a sheep and the Lord is your Good Shepherd?

# Daily Prayer

Father in heaven, thank You for being our Good Shepherd. We really are a lot like sheep, and we desperately need You. We need Your guidance and Your protection. Help us to follow You and not to wander away from the flock. I'm thankful that if we do wander off, You care enough to search for us and bring us back. Thank You that we are safe in Your arms and that no enemy can take us from You. Thank You that we can have a relationship with You and that You love us so much. Help us to be content knowing that You are our shepherd and that You are all we need. Help us to be loyal to You and not to listen to "false shepherds." Thank You most of all that You cared enough about Your sheep to lay down Your life for them. You truly are the Good Shepherd!

# Sixteen

# The Greater Exodus

The Exodus is one of my favorite Old Testament stories, and I love how it points us to an even greater Exodus. God's people, the Israelites, were held bondage by the Egyptians for four hundred years. The Lord sent Moses to lead the people out of slavery. Pharaoh refused to let the people go, so the Lord sent plagues. When the pharaoh still refused to let the people go, God sent the worst plague: every firstborn child would die. But the Lord saved those who had the blood of a lamb on their door post. After this plague, Pharaoh let the people go, but he pursued after them with his army. But the Lord made a way for the Israelites through the Red Sea and destroyed Pharaoh's army. God led them through the desert to the land He had promised.

This story points us to the gospel in so many ways. We weren't slaves to a nation, but we were slaves to sin. It was four hundred years before God sent Moses to deliver the Israelites from slavery. That's a long time. But it would be an even longer time until God sent their true Savior, Jesus Christ. About 1,500 years! Moses instructed the Israelites to slay a spotless lamb, and to put the blood of the lamb on their doorpost in order to be saved from the worst plague. Those who simply believed Moses and put the blood of a spotless lamb on their doorpost were saved from the plague. This pointed to Jesus whose blood saves all who simply believe in Him. Jesus is "the lamb of God who takes away the sin of the world" (John 1:29 NIV). His blood cleanses us of our sins and saves us from the punishment that we deserve: death and eternal separation from God.

Just as the Lord led the Israelites on their journey to the Promised Land, He leads us as well. His Spirit leads us and guides us. Asaph said in Psalm 73:23–24 (NIV), "I am always with you; you hold me by my right hand. You guide me with your counsel, and afterward you will take me into glory." God never left Asaph, even when Asaph was struggling with doubts. Rather, God guided Asaph and helped him recover from his doubts.

The enemy still pursues us. He pursued Asaph and He pursued the Israelites, even after they had been delivered from slavery. We as believers have been freed from our sins, and we are safe in the arms of Christ. But Satan will do anything to try to destroy a believer's faith, whether it be sickness, depression, or whispering lies into our ears. But just as the Lord parted the sea for the Israelites, making a way for them to escape their enemy, He makes a way for us as well. "The Lord says, I will guide you along the best pathway for your life. I will advise you and watch over you" (Psalm 32:8 NLT). The enemy may pursue us and try to destroy us, but just as God destroyed the Egyptian army in the Red Sea, Satan will one day be "thrown into the lake of burning sulfur" (Revelation 20:10 NIV). And remember that God will not allow Satan to destroy us. We are His children, and Jesus said, "No one can snatch them out of my hand" (John 10:28 NIV).

When Moses went up the mountain to pray, he was taking a long time, and the Israelites decided to make an idol. How quick they were to forget about all that God had done for them and to lose hope of what lay ahead! It can feel like God is taking a long time to answer our prayers, and it can feel like Jesus is taking a long time to return. Let us not be like the Israelites but let us stand strong in our faith and "wait patiently for him." Let us look back to all that He has done for us and look forward to our glorious future. Let us trust that He is good and that He will keep His promises, no matter how long it might take.

God promised the Israelites that He would give them the land of Canaan. They had seen so many miracles and evidence for God, yet they still didn't believe that He could help them defeat the Canaanites. We often have doubts as well. We wonder if God can heal us. We wonder if He even cares. We wonder if He is truly with us, and if He truly has our best interest in mind. The Israelites' unbelief led to them spending forty years in the wilderness. God did not abandon His people during the forty years of wandering in the wilderness. He cared for them and met their needs, even though they grumbled often.

We are often the same way. We grumble about many things—sickness, our jobs, other people, etc.—but God does not leave us or forsake us. When the Israelites were hungry and Moses asked God for help, God said, "I will rain down bread from heaven for you" (Exodus 16:4 NIV). This bread was a lifesaver to them and sustained them in the wilderness. In John 6:51 (NIV), Jesus said, "I am the living bread that came down from heaven." Anyone who receives Jesus is saved spiritually and has everlasting life. Moses interceded for the Israelites. He said to them, "You have committed a great sin. But now I will go up to the Lord; perhaps I can make atonement for your sin" (Exodus 32:30 NIV). Jesus intercedes for believers. And it isn't a "perhaps He can make atonement for our sins." He *does* make atonement for our sins because He took the punishment of our sins upon Himself and imputed His righteousness to us!

The Israelites were not at home in the wilderness, but they were looking forward to the day that they would enter the Promised Land.

1 Peter 2:11 (KJV) says that we are "strangers and pilgrims" in this world. This life is a journey, and many times it is hard. But God walks with us and takes care of all our needs. Thanks to Jesus, we have been freed from our bondage, and we are on our way to our Promised Land! Let us not lose sight of what He's done, what He's doing for us, and what He has in store for us.

1. Does waiting during a trial ever cause you to lose sight of what God has done in the past and what He has in store for you?

2. Does your suffering cause you to grumble often as the Israelites did?

# Daily Prayer

Father in heaven, it's so amazing how the Old Testament points to You and the gospel. The Exodus is one of the clearest examples of that. Thank You, Lord, for sending Jesus to free us from the bondage of sin. Help us to remember all that You've done so that we could be saved and have eternal life. And help us to never lose hope of what lies ahead. Help us to trust that You are always with us and that You will meet our needs. Help us to trust that You will lead us and guide us in this life. Help us to trust that You keep Your promises. Help us not to lose sight of You or to grumble against You as the Israelites did. Lord, just as it took Moses a long time to come down from the mountain, sometimes it takes a long time for our prayers to be answered, and it can seem as if You are taking a long time to return. During this time, let us continue to trust in You and help us not to waver in our faith or lose hope. Thank You for all You've done for us, are now doing for us, and for the glorious Promised Land that awaits us!

# Seventeen

## PSALM 44

As I talked about in an earlier devotion, many churches wrongly teach that if you are a believer, then you will not suffer. They teach that if you are walking with God, doing good deeds, and being generous, then you will never suffer, but you will be blessed. While it is true that all believers are blessed, this doesn't mean that we will not suffer in this life, or that we will have health and wealth. We are blessed because we have been saved from our sins, we have a relationship with God, and we have a glorious eternity to look forward to. But as we saw in an earlier devotion, almost every believer mentioned in the Bible suffered. Christians who are walking with God still suffer in this life, and I believe that Psalm 44 teaches this clearly.

In the opening verses, the writer praises God for all that He's done for Israel in the past. He knows that it was by God's mighty hand that the children of Israel were freed from slavery and brought into the land that they now possessed. Next, the writer starts to talk about the present circumstance. He and the Israelites are going through a very hard time. Israel's armies have just been defeated by the enemies, and now the Israelites have been scattered. The writer feels shame and disgrace. He is confused. He doesn't understand why God has allowed this. He then begins to pray. He isn't afraid to express his thoughts and questions to God. He says, "All of this happened to us, *though we had not forgotten you; we had not been false to your covenant. Our hearts had not turned back; our feet had not strayed from your path*" (Psalm 44:17 NIV; emphasis added). He knows that in the past, Israel had been defeated or punished *because* they turned their backs on God, but in this situation, that was not the case. The Israelites had been walking with God, and they were staying faithful to His covenant. Perhaps the writer believed, as do many today, that God should not have allowed suffering because the Israelites had not turned their backs on God.

He goes on in his prayer to say, "Why do you hide your face and forget our misery?" (Psalm 24:44 NIV). He felt forgotten and unloved, as we do many times when we are suffering. But regardless of whether or not he understood why this was happening, and regardless of his feelings, he still chose to put his trust in God. He said, "Rescue us because of your unfailing love" (Psalm 44:26 NIV). He knew that God would never abandon them, and He knew that God would never stop loving them. He knew that God had done great things for them in the past, and he trusted that God would continue to do so. He chose to trust in God no matter how bad the situation looked.

In Romans 8:36 (NIV), Paul quotes a verse from Psalm 44. "For your sake, we face death all day long; we are considered as sheep to be slaughtered." Paul was trying to explain to the Roman church that suffering has always been an experience of God's people, not only in the past but also in the present. But Paul goes on to talk about how even though we may experience suffering and defeat in this world, "the overwhelming victory is ours through Christ" (Romans 8:37 NLT). Christ has defeated Satan, and one day, we will no longer experience suffering. Paul then talks about

God's unfailing love (as the psalmist did). He said, *"Nothing* in all creation will ever be able to separate us from the love of God that is revealed in Jesus Christ our Lord" (Romans 8:39 NLT; emphasis added).

Perhaps you're a Christ follower and you are going through a difficult trial. Maybe you've felt confused or discouraged because you've heard the lies that if you're walking with God, you won't suffer but will only see blessings. Don't listen to this lie, but listen to God's Word, which is true. Remember Psalm 44. Remember how they had remained faithful to God, yet they still experienced great suffering and defeat. We've seen that nearly every believer in the Bible suffered, yet God was with them through it all and He never stopped loving them.

As Paul explained to the Romans, the same goes for believers today. We will still suffer, but the ultimate victory is ours as we've been delivered from our sins and have eternal life, where there will be no more pain because of Christ! No suffering or trial can separate us from His great love. When we are suffering, let us follow the example of the writer of Psalm 44. Let us praise God for all that He's done for us in the past. The writer of Psalm 44 looked back and praised God for freeing the Israelites from slavery and giving them the Promised Land. We can look back and see what Christ has done for us: freed us from the bondage of our sins and given us an eternal home in heaven! Let us also pray. It's OK to bring your questions to God and to tell Him that you don't understand, as the psalmist did. Maybe, like the writer of this psalm, you feel abandoned or unloved. But choose to trust that God will never abandon you. Continue to pray and continue to trust in His plan and in His unfailing love that *nothing* can separate you from.

1.  Have you ever believed that Christians won't suffer but then gone through suffering or watch a loved one suffer? What was your response?

2.  When you go through a trial, do you remember all that God has done for you in the past and believe that He will continue to be good to you? Do you present your thoughts and requests to him?

# Daily Prayer

Father in heaven, thank You for this reminder from Your Word, that even faithful believers who have not strayed from You will still suffer hardships. Even though we may feel defeated in this life, the victory is ours through Christ! When we go through difficult times, help us not to despair but to follow the example of the psalmist. Help us to look back and remember all that You've done for us. Help us to trust that You do not abandon Your people, and You will continue to take care of us, even if it doesn't feel that way. You know what's best for us, and You work all things for our good. Help us to present our thoughts and requests to You. It's OK to tell You that we don't understand. Help us to remember that Your love for us is unfailing and that nothing will separate us from that great love.

# Eighteen

## God Is in Control

As humans, we tend to like to be in control of things. We have a plan for our lives, and we want things to go according to the way we planned them to go. We usually think that we know what is best for our lives. How many times though have things been out of our control or not gone the way that we planned them to go? I don't think that anyone plans on losing their job, finding out they have a disease, or losing a loved one unexpectedly. In our eyes, it would be better if these things didn't happen. Maybe you've been praying for years to be healed of a disease because you believe that life would be better without this disease, and you believe that *right now* is the time for healing. But we have to remember and trust that God knows what is best for us, and His timing is always perfect.

We may not understand how a bad thing could be what's best for us, but we don't know what God has in store, or how God could use it for our good. I think of when Jesus told His disciples that He would have to suffer "and that He must be killed and on the third day raised to life" (Matthew 16:21 NIV). To Peter, this sounded like a bad idea. He said, "Never Lord! This shall never happen to you" (Matthew 16:22 NIV). Peter thought that he knew what was best. But Jesus said, "Get behind me, Satan! *You do not have in mind the concerns of God, but merely human concerns*" (Matthew 16:23 NIV; emphasis added). God knew what was best, not Peter. He knew that through his suffering, death, and resurrection, all humankind could be saved if they believed in him. Sometimes, Satan whispers lies into our ears too, such as *you've had this disease for so long. Maybe God has forgotten about you or is punishing you. Life isn't going the way you planned it to go. Maybe you should just give up or lose hope.* When you hear these lies, you must rebuke them and say, *you don't know what God has in mind.*

I'm sure that Joseph had not planned for his life to go the way that it did, but God had a plan for him—a good plan for him to one day become a great leader and save the land from famine. When Joseph's brothers, who had sold him into slavery, came to him for food, Joseph said, "You intended to harm me, but God intended it for good to accomplish what is now being done, the saving of many lives" (Genesis 50:20 NIV). I think about how this story points to Jesus. Jesus suffered, but it led to Him being the Savior of the world.

Believers make plans for their lives, and there is nothing wrong with that. But ultimately it is God who is in control of our lives. Proverbs 16:9 (NLT) says, "We can make our plans, but the Lord determines our steps." And James 4:13-15 (NIV) says, "Now listen, you who say, "'Today or tomorrow we will go to this or that city, spend a year there, carry on business and make money.' Why, you do not even know what will happen tomorrow. What is your life? You are a mist that appears for a little while and then vanishes. Instead, you ought to say, 'If it is the Lord's will, we will live and do this or that.'"

I never planned to have epilepsy, or that it would worsen and that I wouldn't be able to drive for years. I never planned to struggle with OCD, depression, and anxiety, but I trust that it is God who has allowed me to go through these trials, and I trust that His plan for my life is good. I know that I can only see it from a human perspective, but God sees it in a whole different way. I trust that one day I'll look back and understand why He allowed me to go through this. In Psalm 139:16 (NIV), David says, "Your eyes saw my unformed body; all the days ordained for me were written in your book before one of them came to be." I'm sure that David, a shepherd boy, never planned on one day becoming a great king of Israel, and I'm sure that he never planned on spending much of his life in hiding from the enemies who were pursuing him. But God had a plan for David. He turned a shepherd boy into a great king from whose lineage would come the Son of God, and He used David's time in hiding to allow him to write many of the encouraging psalms that we read today.

Just as God had a plan for Joseph and David's lives, He has a plan for our lives as well. All of our days were "ordained before one of them came to be." God has a plan for each of us, and God's plans will certainly come to pass. Let us trust that God's plan for our life is what's best. If life isn't going the way that you had planned or if you are going through a difficult season, remember that this is part of God's story for your life. He can see the future, and He will use anything that we go through for our good. Let us not be believers who try to control every situation or who get discouraged when things don't go the way that we had planned or when prayers seem to be going unanswered. Rather, let us humbly say like David did, "I trust in you Lord; I say, you are my God. *My times are in your hands*" (Psalm 31:14–15 NIV; emphasis added).

1. Has your life gone according to the way you planned, or have unexpected trials interfered with your plan?

2. Do you trust that God has a plan for your life and that His plans for you are better than your plans, even if His plans involve suffering?

# Daily Prayer

Father in heaven, thank You that You are in control of our lives and that the days ordained for us were written in Your book. Help us not to be believers who always think that we know what's best. Rather, help us to trust that You know what is best for our lives. Lord, when things seem out of our control or don't go the way that we had planned, help us to trust that You are in our story. Even if things get really difficult and we don't understand how this could be good for us, help us to continue to trust in You. You are a God of love, and all Your ways are perfect. Help us to humbly say like David did, "I trust you Lord; my times are in your hands."

# Nineteen

## Our Worth

Have you ever had days, or gone through seasons, when you feel like you have no value or worth? In today's culture, it can be easy, even for Christians, to believe that lie. I believe that's one of the reasons why suicide rates have spiked over the last decade. With social media, we tend to compare our lives to others. And then there's the "likes" and the comments on social media. I know that I would get really upset because it seemed as if everyone else received more "likes" and comments than me. It led me to believe that no one cared about me or my life.

Our culture tends to look up to the wealthy, the attractive, the extroverts, people with a lot of talent, etc. Maybe you are just middle class, or maybe you don't even know where your next meal will come from. Maybe you see all of these beautiful people on television and wish that you could look that way. Maybe you're an introvert and you aren't the life of the party. Maybe you don't have a lot of friends. Maybe you feel like you don't have any talent or anything special to offer people. The world may tell you that you aren't special or worth anything. The world might look down on you. And it's *so easy* to care about what the world thinks. But we have to remember how beautiful and valuable we are in the eyes of God.

I think of the story of David. David was one of eight brothers. God had told the prophet Samuel to go to their home because one of these men was to be the next king of Israel. Samuel was to anoint the one that God had chosen. When Samuel went to their home, he first saw David's seven older brothers. They were tall, strong, fine-looking men. Eliab was the oldest, so Samuel thought, "Surely the Lord's anointed stands here before the Lord. But the Lord said to Samuel, 'Do not consider his appearance or his height, for I have rejected him. *The Lord does not look at the things people look at. People look at the outward appearance, but the Lord looks at the heart'*" (1 Samuel 16:6-7 NIV; emphasis added). After this, their father, Jesse, had each of David's older brothers pass before Samuel to see if they were the one that God had chosen. But God had not chosen any of them.

The Lord had chosen David, the one son that *the people would have least expected* to be chosen. David was just a small, young shepherd boy. He wasn't anything special in the eyes of the world. But in God's eyes, David was very special. David was "a man after God's own heart," and God had big plans for him. He would kill the giant, Goliath. He would become a great king of Israel. He would write many of the psalms we read today. And Jesus, the Messiah, would be a descendant of David. When Jesus walked the earth, many people even called Him "the Son of David."

Maybe in the world's eyes, you are no one special, and this has made you feel unvaluable or worthless. But if you are a believer in Christ, you are *so valuable* in God's eyes! You are His beloved child. He sees you as someone who is beautiful and flawless, not because of anything you've done but because of what Christ has done for us. "He has reconciled you by Christ's physical body through death to present you *holy in his sight, without blemish and free from accusation*" (Colossians 1:22 NIV; emphasis added). It's amazing to think that God sees us this way and that He calls us His children.

Remind yourself to focus less on what the world thinks about you, and more on what God thinks about you. Focus more on your heart than on your outward appearance and status. Just as God had a plan for David's life, He has a plan for yours as well. You might think, *Well, yeah, but I'll never be a great ruler like David was.* Did you know that the Bible says, "The Lord's people will judge the world" (1 Corinthians 6:2 NIV)? And Revelation 2:26 (NIV) says, "To the one who is victorious and does my will to the end, I will give authority over the nations." That's amazing to think about! You may not feel valuable. You may base your value on what the world thinks. But remember what God thinks. Remember how valuable you are to him and how much he loves you. Remember that he has big plans for you.

1. Do you ever feel worthless or unvaluable? Why or why not?

2. Do you tend to base your worth and value on what the world thinks about you or on what God thinks about you?

# $\mathcal{D}$aily $\mathcal{P}$rayer

Father in heaven, thank You that You don't look at the things that people look at. Rather, You look at the heart. Those who have put their faith in You are so loved and valued by You, and You will never let us go. Lord, it is so easy to care about what the world thinks and to become discouraged. Help us to be believers who place our worth and value on what *You* think, not on what the world thinks. Help us to remember to focus more on our hearts than on our outward appearance or status. Help us to have hearts that desire to please you. Help us to remember that just as You had big plans for David's life, You have plans for our lives as well. Thank You for Your amazing love and grace!

# Twenty

## A Crushed Spirit

"The human spirit can endure in sickness, but a crushed spirit who can bear?" (Proverbs 18:14 NIV). When a person is physically sick, whether it be something as simple as a cold or severe as cancer, they may feel awful physically, but they can still be filled with joy and motivation. Even if they are unable to leave the bed, they can still have a strong desire to live, and they can look forward to what they're going to do when they recover. They're motivated to battle their sickness, and they do everything they can to beat it. But a crushed spirit is different from a physical sickness. When the Bible speaks of a crushed spirit, I believe it is speaking of depression.

Depression is more than just being sad because of a circumstance. When people are sad, there is normally a reason behind the sadness (e.g., death of a loved one or watching a child go through an illness). But depression is "a mood disorder that causes a persistent feeling of sadness and loss of interest" (Mayo Clinic). Depression doesn't always have a reason. I've lived with epilepsy for seventeen years. Though this has never been easy, I was still happy, and I still enjoyed life. I was motivated to do things, including doing everything that I could to beat epilepsy. But several years ago, I was diagnosed with major depressive disorder. It was a struggle just to get out of bed every morning. I had no motivation or desire to do anything. I felt sad for no reason. Life seemed more like a struggle than a joy.

Depression tries to steal your joy, your hope, and your motivation. In these dark times, it can be harder to feel God's love and presence. But He hasn't left your side, and He cares about you more than anyone else. In fact, Psalm 34:18 (ESV) says, "The Lord is near to the broken hearted and saves the crushed in spirit." God understands depression more than anyone. Hebrews 4:15 (NIV) says, "We do not have a high priest who is unable to empathize with our weaknesses, but we have one who has been tempted in every way, just as we are- yet he did not sin." Jesus experienced all of the emotions that we experience, including sadness and sorrow. In John 11, we read of Jesus weeping over the death of Lazarus. In Luke 19:41, He wept over the city of Jerusalem. In the garden of gethsemane, Jesus said, "My soul is *crushed* with grief to the point of death" (Matthew 26:38 NLT; emphasis added).

Jesus experienced deep sorrow. Isaiah tells us that the Messiah would be a *man of sorrows and acquainted with grief.* But Jesus never gave up or lost hope. Hebrews 12:2 (NIV; emphasis added) says, *"For the joy set before him*, he endured the cross, scorning it's shame and sat down at the right hand of the throne of God." He endured sorrow and suffering because he had hope of what was ahead. And because of his endurance, He now sits at the right hand of God, and He is our King and our Savior forever.

How comforting it is to know that Jesus understands how we feel and that He has compassion for us. Let us be like Christ and not lose hope of what God has planned for us. Let us not lose sight of eternity where there will be no more sorrow. Let us endure through the trial of depression and sorrow, knowing that our Savior is walking through the fire with us. Spurgeon said this: "God is good. He will not forsake you: He will bear you through ... Everything else will fail, but His Word never will."

Perhaps you believe that God is upset with you for feeling this way, that he doesn't understand, or that you can only approach Him when you feel good, but this is far from the truth. Spurgeon was one of the greatest preachers of all time, yet he suffered depression for much of his life. He said this in one of his sermons: "I desire to speak as a weak and suffering preacher, of that High Priest who is full of compassion: and my longing is that any who are low in spirit, faint, or despondent, and even out of the way, may take heart to approach the Lord Jesus. Jesus is touched, not with a feeling of your strength, but of your infirmity. Down here, poor, feeble nothings affect the heart of their great High Priest who is crowned with glory and honor. As the mother feels with the weakness of her babe, so does Jesus feel with the poorest, saddest, and weakest of his chosen."

1. Have you ever experienced depression? If so, how did you react to the sorrow?

2. When struggling with depression, do you ever believe that God is upset with you or that He doesn't understand? Do you still choose to run to Him in faith?

# Daily Prayer

Father in heaven, depression can be one of the hardest things to go through. Help us, when we are depressed, to run to You in faith, knowing that You are full of compassion. Help us to know that You haven't left our side. Rather, the Bible says that You *"are near* to the broken hearted." Lord, You understand depression more than anyone, and You even experienced much grief and sorrow, perhaps even depression. It can be easy when feeling depressed to lose sight of what lies ahead. Help us to be like You and to remember the joy that awaits us in heaven. Help us to endure the trial of depression, knowing that You are by our side, You care, and You will see us through.

# Twenty-one

## Depression in the Bible?

As I talked about in the previous devotion, depression can be a very difficult thing to deal with. It may be circumstantial, or it might not. Spurgeon said in one of his sermons, "You may have no outward cause for sorrow and yet if the mind is dejected, the brightest sunshine will not relieve your gloom. There are times when all our evidence gets clouded and all our joys are fled. Though we may still cling to the cross, yet it is with a desperate grasp." I know that this has been true of my depression. I cling to Jesus and His Word, but sometimes it is with desperate grasp. Depression has tried to steal my peace and joy. It's tried to steal my motivation. It's led to doubts. And the enemy wants me to believe that God has left me, that He is angry at me, that a Christian shouldn't be depressed. But this is so far from the truth!

As we talked about in the devotion before, "He is *near* to the broken hearted and *saves* the crushed in spirit." And it pleases God if I just come to Him even with a desperate grasp, saying, "Lord, I feel awful. I'm struggling to feel Your love and presence. I'm having doubts. Please help me!" And I believe it's the Holy Spirit who helps us endure through depression and who helps us to continue clinging to Christ and His Word.

Depressed believers may feel guilty for feeling the way they do. They may even be shamed by other believers who tell them that they shouldn't be depressed or that they just don't have enough faith. The thought that my depression was a sin or that maybe I just didn't have enough faith would bother me terribly. I began to think that, as a Christian, I should always have joy and that if I'm depressed, something must be wrong. Spurgeon said this as well: "Depression of spirit is no index of declining grace—the very loss of joy and the absence of assurance may be accompanied by the greatest advancement in the spiritual life." Depression might be a trial in which God is refining us like gold. It also gives us the opportunity to endure in our faith. Did you know that many believers in the Bible had to endure sadness, despair, and perhaps what we would call depression? Let's take a look at a few of them.

The great prophet Elijah was threatened by Queen Jezebel, so he fled into the wilderness in fear. He sat down under a tree, worn and discouraged, and he prayed, "I have had enough, Lord. Take my life, I am not better than my ancestors. Then he lay under the bush and fell asleep" (1 Kings 19:4–5 NIV). Then there's King David. David speaks of his anguish in many of the psalms. He says, "Why are you cast down, O my soul, and why are you in turmoil within me?" (Psalm 42:5 ESV). David also wrote, "How long must I wrestle with my thoughts and day after day have sorrow in my heart?" (Psalm 13:2 NIV).

There's also Job, the man who lost his wealth, his health, and his family. He is so miserable that he says, "Why did I not perish at birth, and die as I came from the womb?" (Job 3:11 NIV). He also says, "I have no rest, but only turmoil" (Job 3:26 NIV). In Job 10:1 (NIV) he says, "I loathe my very life." Jeremiah was known as "the weeping prophet." He was a man of great faith, but the people's constant rejection of his message led him to despair. He said, "Cursed be the day I was born!" (Jeremiah 20:14 NIV). In the New Testament, we talked about how even our Lord Jesus experienced deep grief and sorrow. Then there's the apostle Paul. 2 Corinthians 1:8 (NIV) says that he "despaired of life itself" because of his afflictions.

All of these men had to endure great sorrow, but God never abandoned them. We can even look at modern times and see great men of faith who suffered depression. As I've mentioned before, Charles Spurgeon, who was known as "the prince of preachers," battled depression for much of his life. But he believed that his depression was ordained by God, for God's glory and for his own sanctification. I too believe that God can use depression to help sanctify us and draw us closer to Him. In my depression, I've spent more time in His Word as I seek comfort and seek to learn what God has to say about depression. I was amazed to discover that sorrow was very common among many saints. And while my prayers aren't always long and lengthy in seasons of depression, I believe they are more genuine as I've cried out to God for comfort and relief.

Spurgeon said, "When we see people from the Bible like Elijah, who wanted to die, and the Psalmist, who wrestled with depression and feelings of abandonment by God, and we find ourselves in similar places, we are relieved by discovering that we are walking along a path which others have traversed before us. We see these saints cast into darkness. We see God's faithfulness. We see God's promises that are strong enough to hold them—and us as well. Don't be dismayed, their stories remind us. This is a trial many have had to endure. You are still His. The Christ who bought you will not abandon you in the dark."

So, if you ever believe that a Christian should never experience depression, or that a depressed Christian just doesn't have enough faith, remind yourself of these great saints. Remind yourself that you are walking along a path that they had to walk on as well. And remind yourself that God loves you, and He will see you through.

1. Have you ever been told, or believed, that your depression is a sin or a lack of faith? How did you react to this?

2. Does it bring you relief to know that many saints of God have had to endure depression and that God saw each of them through?

# Daily Prayer

Father in heaven, thank You for Your Word, where we can discover that we are not alone in our troubles. We read about many believers who suffered with deep sorrow and depression. Lord, help this knowledge to bring comfort to believers who experience depression. It can be easy, when we are depressed, to believe the lie that we aren't supposed to be depressed as Christians or that we are sinning. But Your Word makes it clear that Christians are not exempt from depression. Charles Spurgeon even believed that You ordained his depression. And it's very possible that You've ordained it for many of us as well, in order to use it for something good. Lord, it's also easy to feel abandoned by You when we are depressed but help us to remember that just as You were faithful to all of these believers that we talked about, You will be faithful to us as well. You are "near to the broken hearted."

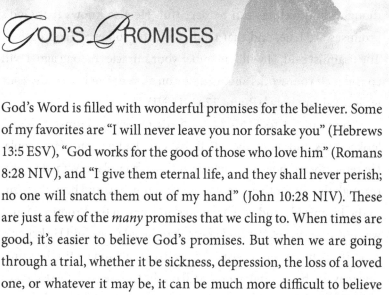

# Twenty-two

# God's Promises

God's Word is filled with wonderful promises for the believer. Some of my favorites are "I will never leave you nor forsake you" (Hebrews 13:5 ESV), "God works for the good of those who love him" (Romans 8:28 NIV), and "I give them eternal life, and they shall never perish; no one will snatch them out of my hand" (John 10:28 NIV). These are just a few of the *many* promises that we cling to. When times are good, it's easier to believe God's promises. But when we are going through a trial, whether it be sickness, depression, the loss of a loved one, or whatever it may be, it can be much more difficult to believe God's promises. Consider the writer of Psalm 77. He was in deep distress, and his prayers seemed to be going unanswered. He said, "Will the Lord reject forever? Will he never show his favor again? Has his unfailing love vanished forever? *Has his promise failed for all time?* Has God forgotten to be merciful? Has he in anger withheld his compassion?" (Psalm 77:7–9 NIV; emphasis added).

Because of the psalmist's difficult situation, he was beginning to question God and God's promises. So many times when believers are going through trials, we experience the same thoughts. Praying every day for seventeen years for healing, but not seeing any change, has certainly put very similar thoughts into my head. Depression

101

has also put these thoughts into my head. I'm sure the enemy uses several situations to put these thoughts into believers' minds. He doesn't want us to believe in God's promises. He wants us to be discouraged and to question God and His Word. But let's look at what the psalmist does next. He chooses to reject his thoughts and feelings and cling to what he knows to be true. He *knows* that his thoughts and feelings can be deceitful. He also knows that God's promises are true, and that God is faithful to keep His promises. The psalmist said, "I will remember your miracles of long ago. I will consider all your works and meditate on all your mighty deeds. Your ways, God, are holy" (Psalm 77:11–13 NIV).

The psalmist took his eyes off his present circumstance and looked back and remembered all that God had done for His people. He remembered how God delivered them from slavery, made a way through the sea for them, took care of their needs, and brought them to the Promised Land. The Israelites' journey to the Promised Land was not an easy one, but God never abandoned them, and He kept his promises. The writer of the psalm realizes that God is still the same. Life may not be easy, but God is still on the throne, and He still takes care of us and keeps His promises.

It's easy, when we are suffering, to only focus on ourselves and our problems, but the psalmist chooses to focus on God. His thoughts and feelings were telling him that perhaps God had abandoned him, perhaps God's love had failed, and perhaps the Lord had no compassion for him. But the writer knew that these thoughts were not true. The writer knew the promises of God and he knew that the Lord kept His promises. He knew that God is holy and that God cannot break His promises.

Let's consider some of the promises that God has fulfilled. He promised Abraham a son and to make a great nation come from him. He gave Abraham a son, Isaac, and the nation of Israel descended from him. He promised Noah that a flood would destroy the earth, which did take place, but then He also promised to never flood the earth again. He promised to deliver the Israelites from slavery and to give them the Promised Land. God promised Israel that after being scattered among the nations, they would one day become a nation again, and we saw this fulfilled in 1948.

But most importantly, He promised to send us a Savior. The first promise of a Savior is seen in Genesis 3:15 (NIV), which says, "He will crush your head." This speaks of Jesus's victory over Satan. And that promise was fulfilled through Christ's death and resurrection. Even though it was nearly 4,000 years after the promise, God did not forget His promise or abandon it. Jesus promised to return to earth, and even though it's been 2,000 years, we can be certain that He will keep this promise as well. We can be sure that *every* promise for us in God's Word is true. Sometimes God may take longer than we hope or expect, but we can trust that His timing is best and that His promises will never fail. Joshua 21:45 (NIV) says, "Not one of all the Lord's good promises to Israel failed. Every one was fulfilled."

The Lord cannot lie. When we start to doubt His promises, let us be like the psalmist and choose to reject our thoughts and cling to the promises of God, which are true. Let us take our eyes off our present circumstances and look to all that God has done for us, and all He has in store for us. Hebrews 10:23 (NIV; emphasis added) says, "Let us hold unswervingly to the hope we profess, for *he who promised is faithful*." When the Lord promised Sarah a child in her old age, her thoughts were telling her that it wasn't possible; she had doubts. But she knew that God's promise would be fulfilled. "She considered him *faithful* who had made the promise" (Hebrews 11:11 NIV; emphasis added). And she did indeed have a child.

So, no matter how hard your situation, what your thoughts are telling you, or how long you've been going through a trial, choose to believe in God's wonderful promises. Charles Spurgeon said, "When we are flailing about, when we don't know if we can go on, when we feel lost, when the darkness consumes us, *we cling to God's promises, even when we hardly have the strength to believe them. They are sure, regardless of our feelings, regardless of our outward state.*"

1.  Do you ever struggle to believe God's promises? Why or why not?

2.  Do you believe that God's promises are sure, regardless of how you feel or what you're going through?

# Daily Prayer

Father in heaven, thank You for all of Your wonderful promises. And thank You that they are sure, regardless of our feelings or circumstances. Sometimes when we are going through difficult times, it can be a struggle to believe Your promises. We may ask questions like the psalmist did. But like the psalmist, we can look back and see what You have done. We know that You are faithful, and we know that You are good. We know that You keep Your promises and that You cannot lie. Help us to always choose to believe the promises that You've given us in Your Word. Our hearts can be deceiving, but Your Word is holy and true, and it never changes.

# Twenty-three

## JEHOSHAPHAT

Have you ever been in a situation where you don't know what to do? Maybe you've lost your job and don't know how you're going to pay the bills or where your next meal will come from. Maybe you're fighting a disease and you've done everything you could do to get better, but things are only getting worse. Or maybe you've even been told that you only have a short amount of time left to live. Maybe you're battling depression, and you don't know how you're going to make it through the day. Or maybe you just have a big decision to make, and you don't know what to do.

In 2 Chronicles, we read about a king named Jehoshaphat who was in a situation where he didn't know what to do. He was told that a vast army was on their way to destroy him and his people. Chapter 20:3 (ESV) says, "Then Jehoshaphat was afraid and set his face to seek the Lord." Being afraid is a normal human reaction in these types of situations. It's normal to feel afraid when you lose your job or when you find out that you or a loved one has a disease. But as believers, we know who to turn to when we are feeling afraid. And we know that we do not need to fear because our God is greater than anything that we might be facing, and He is on our side.

Jehoshaphat humbled himself in the presence of God and the

people. He admitted that he didn't know what to do. But he knew that God is all-powerful. He remembered all that God had done for the people in the past, and he knew that God could do it again. "He ordered everyone in Judah to begin fasting. So people from all the towns of Judah came to Jerusalem to seek the Lord's help" (2 Chronicles 20:3-4 NLT).

In 2 Chronicles 20:12 (NIV), he prayed, "We have no power to face this vast army that is attacking us. We do not know what to do, but our eyes are on you." A man named Jahaziel came to Jehoshaphat and said, "This is what the Lord says to you: do not be afraid or discouraged because of this vast army. For the battle is not yours, but God's ... you will not have to fight this battle. Take up your positions; stand firm and see the deliverance the Lord will give you" (2 Chronicles 20:15-17 NIV). So, the next morning they headed out to meet the enemies. "When the men of Judah came to the place that overlooks the desert and looked toward the vast army, they saw only dead bodies lying on the ground; no one had escaped" (2 Chronicles 20:24 NIV).

We can learn several things from this story. First, Jehoshaphat, being a king, could have let his pride get in the way. He may have thought, *I'll figure out a way to do this on my own. I don't want to tell the people that I don't know what to do.* But he chose to humble himself before God and the people, and he admitted that he didn't know what to do. Proverbs 11:2 (NIV) says, "When pride comes, then comes disgrace, but with the humble is wisdom." Second, he knew who to turn to. He turned to God and asked for help. He knew that only God could help him. He also asked the people to pray. And third, he had enough faith to do as God told him to do.

Jehoshaphat set a great example for us as believers. When we are in a situation where we don't know what to do, we should humble ourselves and turn to God. We should say, "God, I don't know what to do, but I know that you can do all things. Please help me. I trust in you. The battle belongs to you." We shouldn't pretend to know everything or try to do the impossible on our own. Let us humble ourselves, turn our eyes to God, and ask Him for his mighty hand to intervene. Let us also ask others to pray for us. Many times, believers choose not to ask others to pray for them. Maybe it's a pride thing. Maybe they just don't want others to see their flaws. Maybe they're embarrassed of the situation they are going through. But praying for each other is very biblical, as is humbling ourselves. And lastly, let us have faith that the battle is the Lord's and that whatever happens is what's best. Maybe God will reveal Himself in a mighty way like He did for Jehoshaphat and the people of Judah. Or maybe things won't turn out the way you had hoped. This doesn't change the fact that God hears our prayers, He cares, He is all-powerful, and He is in control. Sometimes He has a different plan in mind, but we can trust that His way is always best, and that He is working all things together for our good.

1. Have you ever been, or are you currently, in a situation where you don't know what to do?

2. Do you turn to God in these situations and admit that you don't know what to do? Do you ask others to pray for you?

# Daily Prayer

Father in heaven, thank You that when we are in situations that seem hopeless and we don't know what to do, we can turn our eyes to You, and You care. Lord, we know that You are all-powerful and that nothing is impossible with You. You are greater than any battle that we may face. Help us to look back and remember all that You have done and help us to remember that You are the same God today. Help us to be humble and to present our requests to You. Help us not to hesitate to ask others to pray for us as well. And then help us to trust in You. Help us to trust that our battle is in Your hands, and You never fail. Whatever happens, we can trust that it is what's best for us.

# Twenty-four

## Perfect Peace

"You will keep him in perfect peace whose mind is stayed on you, because he trusts in you" (Isaiah 26:3 ESV). This is such a beautiful promise from God's Word. Yet, most believers do not have perfect peace all the time. So many things in this life distract us from our Savior. We shift our focus from God to the worries of this world. And it can be *so easy* to get distracted. We can feel full of faith and peace one minute and the next be filled with fear and doubt. I think about when Peter was walking on the water toward Jesus. He was literally looking right at Jesus, the Son of God. Not only that, but He had witnessed countless miracles that Jesus had done. And now, he himself was part of a miracle—walking on water! He had no reason to fear or to doubt. But he quickly became distracted. He took his eyes off Jesus and began to look at the rough conditions around him. The wind and the waves were strong, and he became afraid. He no longer had complete trust in Jesus. Just like that, his peace was taken away, he began to doubt, and he started to sink.

Peter should have kept his focus on Jesus, and trusted in Jesus, regardless of the rough conditions around him. This would have given him peace. It's easy to point fingers at Peter, but the same thing happens to each of us. Every day, we are surrounded by our own personal wind and waves, things that try to distract us from our Savior. Things that try to steal our peace. And many times, we take our eyes off Jesus and begin to doubt and to fear. Spurgeon said this in one of his sermons: "Peter is at one moment confident, another instant he is dismayed. At one moment he is treading the waves like a miracle worker, and the next instant he is sinking like an ordinary being. And so it is with us- sometimes aloft and soon crying out of the depths, 'Lord, save me.'"

Every day, we should be intentional about keeping our focus on God. This doesn't mean we have to be thinking about Him 24/7. A person "whose mind is stayed on God" is a person whose mind is filled with God's truth. When problems arise, they shift their focus from their problems to God. They trust God to take care of them, and they trust in all His promises. But in order for our minds to be filled with God's truth, we must be intentional about spending time with Him daily in His Word, in prayer, and in praise. The more time we spend with God, the more we know Him, the more we trust Him, and the more our minds are filled with His truth. But even Peter, who spent all day, every day, with Jesus, still became distracted and let fear and unbelief get in the way. Fear and troubles will present themselves many times in our lives, but we must choose to shift our focus from fear and troubles to God and His Word.

Having a seizure disorder, I know how easy it can be for fear to come upon someone. I know how quickly someone's peace can be taken away. I can be like Peter, feeling confident and full of faith one moment and then the next distracted and overcome with fear. Fear and doubts come upon me every day. I must be intentional about taking my mind off the fear and doubts and putting it onto Jesus. Sometimes when fear comes, I'll pray. Other times I'll quote verses from scripture to remind me of God's goodness and His faithfulness. Or sometimes I'll put on a praise and worship song. And I have to remind myself that just as He was right there with Peter, He's also right here with me. I remind myself that He is my Good Shepherd. When I do these things, the fear begins to flee and is suddenly replaced with peace.

When Peter began sinking, he cried out, "Lord, save me! Immediately Jesus reached out his hand and caught him" (Matthew 14:30–31 NIV). Jesus saves us spiritually the moment we ask Him to save us. And when we are going through troubles, we should cry out for Him to help us. We can be assured that He is with us, and that He is our peace. When the troubles of this world come and try to steal your peace and distract you from Christ, be intentional about shifting your focus to Christ. Trust in Him and His promises, and He will give you peace, no matter what your circumstances may be.

1. Do you ever feel like Peter: one minute full of faith and the next full of fear and doubts?

2. Do you notice that you have more peace when you are focused more on God than on life's circumstances?

# Daily Prayer

Father in heaven, thank You that You give perfect peace. Lord, it can be so easy for us to become distracted from You. Just as Peter was distracted by the wind and waves, we have many distractions as well, things that try to bring us fear and doubt. Lord, when this happens, help us to be intentional about shifting our focus back to You and putting our trust in You. Help us to spend time with You daily in Your Word, in prayer, and in praise. Help us to know You more and to trust You more. Help our minds to always be filled with Your truth so that we can have perfect peace, no matter what our circumstances may be.

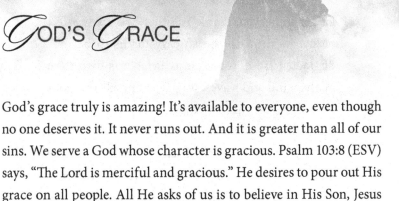

# Twenty-five

## GOD'S GRACE

God's grace truly is amazing! It's available to everyone, even though no one deserves it. It never runs out. And it is greater than all of our sins. We serve a God whose character is gracious. Psalm 103:8 (ESV) says, "The Lord is merciful and gracious." He desires to pour out His grace on all people. All He asks of us is to believe in His Son, Jesus Christ, who died for our sins. "You, Lord, are forgiving and good, abounding in love to all who call to you" (Psalm 86:5 NIV).

To those who put their trust in Jesus, God's grace covers *all* of their sins past, present, and future. It doesn't matter what they've done. His grace is far greater. "Where sin abounded, grace did *much more* abound" (Romans 5:20 KJV; emphasis added). I think of the thief on the cross. He must have committed a pretty awful crime to be sentenced to crucifixion. But he trusted in Jesus in his final moments on the cross, and God's grace was greater than his crime *and* all of his past sins. I think about David, who committed adultery and had a man killed. He repented, and God's grace was greater. I think about the prodigal son. He had everything he needed with his father, yet he chose to walk away from home and spend all of his inheritance on worldly, sinful pleasures. But he realized that he had made a mistake. He said, "I will set out and go back to my father and say to him: Father, I have sinned against heaven and against you" (Luke 15:18 NIV). It wasn't too late; the father's grace hadn't run out. Rather, the father welcomed him with opened arms and showed him love and grace.

In Mark 9 we read about the man who wanted Jesus to heal his son. He said to Jesus, "If you can do anything, take pity on us and help us. 'If you can'? said Jesus. 'Everything is possible for one who believes. Immediately the boy's father exclaimed, 'I do believe; help me overcome my unbelief!'" (Mark 9:22–24 NIV). The father had faith, but he also knew that his faith was far from perfect. He knew that he struggled with doubts. His faith didn't need to be perfect for God to show him grace. As we've talked about in previous devotions, all we need is faith the size of a mustard seed. God's grace was greater than the father's weakness, and Jesus healed his son.

Maybe you have done some things that you really regret. There's *nothing* you have done that God's grace cannot cover. Maybe you've left the church and turned to worldly pleasures as the prodigal son did. Maybe you think it's too late to return to God. But God is waiting for you to return to Him. He longs for you to return. Maybe you think your sins are too great or too numerous for God to forgive. Remember the thief on the cross. And remember that "if we confess our sins, he is faithful and just and will forgive us our sins and purify us from *all unrighteousness* (1 John 1:9 NIV; emphasis added). Maybe you feel discouraged because you battle with sin every day and you fear that God's grace might run out. But praise God, His grace never runs out! Lamentations 3:22 (ESV; emphasis added) says, "His mercies *never* come to an end." Maybe your faith is weak, and you have doubts. This leads you to believe that your faith isn't strong enough to acquire God's grace. But remember the man who cried, "I believe; help my unbelief!"

Satan wants us to doubt God's grace. He wants us to fear that we have not obtained God's grace. But we must remind ourselves of God's gracious character. He desires to pour out His grace on everyone. His grace is so much greater than all of our sins, and His grace never runs out. Spurgeon said, "We dishonor God if we think our sin greater than His grace. God's grace is infinitely greater than the greatest of our crimes." You may not *feel* his grace or *feel* like you've been cleansed from all unrighteousness, but remember our feelings can be very deceitful, while God's Word is always true. Choose to believe God's Word over your feelings. Choose to believe in His *amazing* grace!

1. Have you ever struggled to believe that God's grace is greater than your sins?

2. Have you ever feared that perhaps His grace for you might run out?

# Daily Prayer

Father in heaven, thank You for Your amazing grace, which we don't deserve. Thank You that You are a gracious God eager to pour out Your grace on all who come to You. Even if we only have mustard-sized faith, Your grace is greater than our weakness. Lord, it can be easy to think that our sins are too great or too numerous for Your grace. Help us to resist those lies and to stand firm on the truth of Your Word. Your Word tells us that Your grace is greater than our sins and that Your grace never runs out. Help us to remember that Your grace is a gift to us. It isn't something that we deserve. Help us to be so grateful for Your grace and help us to be like You and show grace to others, even when they don't deserve it.

# Twenty-six

## PERSISTENCE

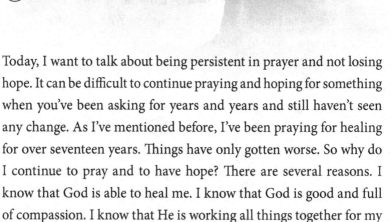

Today, I want to talk about being persistent in prayer and not losing hope. It can be difficult to continue praying and hoping for something when you've been asking for years and years and still haven't seen any change. As I've mentioned before, I've been praying for healing for over seventeen years. Things have only gotten worse. So why do I continue to pray and to have hope? There are several reasons. I know that God is able to heal me. I know that God is good and full of compassion. I know that He is working all things together for my good. *And* because we are taught in His Word to *be persistent.*

In Luke, Jesus gives us the parable of the persistent widow. It starts off by saying, "Jesus told his disciples a parable to show them that they should *always pray and not give up*" (Luke 18:1 NIV; emphasis added). If you've been praying for something or someone for a long time, don't give up! That's exactly what the enemy wants us to do. He wants us to believe that God doesn't hear us, that He doesn't care, that He's abandoned us, or that He'll never answer our prayers...but none of these things are true! In this parable, the widow continued to come to a judge with a plea to "give her justice against her adversary." The judge didn't care about her or her situation, and he didn't care about God or doing the right thing, but eventually, since the widow was persistent and wouldn't give up, the judge finally granted her request. Jesus said, "Listen to what the unjust judge says. And will not God bring about justice for his chosen ones who cry out to him day and night? Will he keep putting them off?" (Luke 18:6–7 NIV).

Just like the persistent widow, we are needy and helpless. Many times, there is nothing that we can do except cry out to God, our righteous Judge. Praise God, we have a Judge who listens to us and one who truly cares about us. Unlike the unjust judge, Jesus *wants* us to come to Him with our pleas. And He doesn't just put us and our problems off to the side as the unjust judge did. He answers our cries for help, in His perfect timing. And Jesus Christ, our righteous Judge, *always makes the best decisions*. He knows what is best, not us, and He will do what is best for us if we trust Him.

In the same parable, Jesus said, "However, when the Son of Man comes, will he find faith on the earth?" (Luke 18:8 NIV). Will Jesus find believers who persistently call out to Him, trusting in Him and His timing? Will He find believers who "wait patiently on the Lord?" Or will Jesus find people who have given up, people who thought prayer was a waste of time? People who believed that God didn't care about them or their problems.

My family had been praying for my grandmother for *several* years. Anytime I would share the gospel with her, she would just laugh and tell me that she's a good person. She didn't believe that Jesus was the only way. One night, my father and I went to visit her at the nursing home. We knew that she didn't have much time left so we shared the gospel with her one last time. To our surprise, she accepted it with joy! She prayed and asked Jesus to be her Savior! Imagine if my family had just given up on praying for her. Things may not have turned out the way they did. It seemed hopeless that she would ever receive Christ, but we chose to be persistent in praying for her, and God answered our prayers *in His timing.*

We find other passages in the Bible that teach us to be persistent in prayer. 1 Thessalonians 5:16–18 (ESV; emphasis added) says, "Rejoice always, *pray without ceasing,* give thanks in all circumstances, for this is the will of God in Christ Jesus for you." We can rejoice and give thanks in *all* circumstances, even if our prayers seem to be going unanswered, because we know that we have a perfect and righteous Judge who sits on the throne. We know that He hears our cries and that He cares about us. We know that whatever He decides for us is what's best for us. We know that if our lives are in His hands, then we have nothing to worry about. God is pleased with those who faithfully seek Him and don't give up but continue to trust in Him and His plan.

Colossians 4:2 (NLT) says, "Devote yourselves to prayer with an alert mind and a thankful heart." Prayer shouldn't be something that we only do if our schedule allows it. Prayer should be high on our priority list. Our prayers should be sincere and from the heart. Not just a quick "There, I said my prayers for the day." I think this is what Paul means when he tells the Colossian believers to pray with an alert mind. When I'm praying with the kids at bedtime and they begin to goof around or talk, I remind them that we are talking to the God of the universe right now. I think sometimes even adults need that reminder. We aren't just talking to the ceiling or mumbling a bunch of unheard words. We are talking to the King of Kings, and He hears us! Amazing that we can have that relationship with Him. So, if you've been praying for something for years, don't give up! Continue to pray, with thanksgiving and with an alert mind. Trust that your righteous judge hears your pleas, and He cares. Trust in His perfect decision for your life.

1. Are you persistent in prayer? Is it difficult to be persistent when your prayers seem to be going unanswered?

2. Is there a prayer you've seen answered after many years of praying?

# Daily Prayer

Father in heaven, thank You that, unlike the unjust judge in the parable of the persistent widow, You are a God who truly cares about us and our needs. Lord, it can be discouraging to continue praying when our prayers seem to be going unanswered. Help us to resist lies from the enemy that try to make us believe that our prayers aren't being heard or that You don't care. Lord, we know that You hear all of our prayers and that You care about us more than we can imagine. Help us to trust that Your timing and Your plan is perfect. Help us to not only be persistent in prayer, but to pray with thanksgiving and with an alert mind because this is Your will for us.

# Twenty-seven

## Overcomers

"You dear children, are from God and have overcome them, because the one who is in you is greater than the one who is in the world" (1 John 4:4 NIV). What an amazing promise! In the context of this verse, there were many false teachers who were trying to deceive the believers. They were trying to get them to doubt their faith and to believe all sorts of lies. Even today, we have *many* false teachers, and we are surrounded by lies, whether it be someone claiming that evolution is true, someone saying that a certain sin, such as abortion or homosexuality is OK, or even a pastor who adds or takes away from God's Word as he preaches. You may even have false thoughts pop into your head often.

We live in a culture where believers are mocked and pressured to be like the world. Every day, we are surrounded by false teachings on TV, the radio, YouTube, billboards, at school, and at work. Maybe these false teachings put questions in your mind. You might feel like David who felt like the enemy was "triumphing over him." But John assured believers that we have overcome all of the lies and sins. How have we overcome? Because of Jesus who defeated *all evil* by His death and resurrection. And because of our faith in Him, His Holy Spirit now lives in us. "The spirit of him who raised Jesus from the dead is living in you" (Romans 8:11 NIV).

Once a person receives Jesus as their Lord and Savior, His Spirit is with them, and He *never* leaves them. His blood has washed us clean, and we now overcome the world and sin because of what Jesus did and because He is with us. His Spirit helps us to endure in the faith. Romans 8:26 (NIV) says, "The Spirit helps us in our weakness." You may recall the verse we talked about in an earlier devotion: "For false messiahs and false prophets will appear and perform great signs and wonders to deceive, *if possible,* even the elect" (Matthew 24:24 NIV). We don't overcome temptations and false teachings by our own strength but because the one who is in us gives us strength. He will not allow any of His children to be deceived. "He who began a good work in you will carry it on to completion until the day of Christ Jesus" (Philippians 1:6 NIV).

The Spirit guides us and helps us to discern whether something is true or not. He gives us strength to say no to sin and to stand up for what's right. We need not fear any evil that comes against us because the one who lives in us is so much greater! Indeed, Jesus has overcome the world, and His children have overcome as well because He has delivered us from evil, and His Spirit lives inside us. But until Jesus returns, the devil is still roaming free, and he hates God's children. He can't steal our salvation. Jesus said that "no one will snatch them out of my hand" (John 10:28 NIV). We've already overcome the enemy because of what Christ did for us. But the devil can certainly still tempt us and fill our minds with lies and with doubts. He would love to get believers to doubt their faith and to keep them from sharing the gospel and from being a light to the world.

1 Peter 5:8-10 (NIV) says, "Be alert and of sober mind. Your enemy the devil prowls around like a roaring lion looking for someone to devour. Resist him, standing firm in the faith, because you know that the family of believers throughout the world is undergoing the same kind of sufferings. And the God of all grace, who called you to

his eternal glory in Christ, after you have suffered a little while, will himself restore you and make you strong, firm and steadfast." This verse tells believers that we have been called to God's eternal glory. It tells us that we will have suffering. But it also tells us that we will overcome. God will help us to endure, and one day we will no longer experience suffering.

The life of a believer is not easy. We live in an anti-Christian world. A world that hates us. A world where there are temptations all around us. A world where we hear all sorts of lies. Believers all around the world are suffering. The devil will use anything he can to try to get them to doubt their faith, whether it be a disease, the death of a loved one, or false teachings. I know that for me, he has used my struggles, especially my OCD, to try to get me to doubt. I've obsessed over thoughts such as *Maybe I'm not a genuine believer. Maybe I can lose my salvation. Is there evidence in my life that shows I've been saved? Why do I not enjoy doing such and such? Shouldn't I want to enjoy those things as a believer?*

My epilepsy and depression have also put doubts and despair into my mind. *Why are You allowing this, Lord? Do You hear my prayers? Do You care? Are you punishing me?* The devil tries to use these things to devour me. But I need not fear these thoughts because the One who lives in me has already had the victory over these things. And I continue to resist these lies and to cling to the truth of God's Word. How do I continue to do it? I don't do it in my own strength but because the Holy Spirit lives in me. He gives me strength to endure. He gives me strength to keep believing. He helps me to discern right from wrong. He is far greater than the enemy.

Of course, I still make mistakes often, but I have been cleansed of *all* my sins by the blood of Christ. I have overcome sin, doubts and obsessive thoughts because of *His* blood. And one day Satan will be "hurled down," and he will no longer be able to tempt us and torture us. Revelation 12:11 (NIV; emphasis added) says that believers "triumphed over him *by the blood of the Lamb and by the word of their testimony.*" So, no matter how difficult things may be, or how dark this world gets, if you are a believer, remember that you have overcome—not because of anything that you've done but because of the one who is in you. He has overcome. And "the one who is in you is greater than the one who is in the world." Anyone who puts their faith in Jesus has been cleansed and has been sealed with the Holy Spirit. They are now overcomers. 1 John 5:5 (NIV) says, "Who is it that overcomes the world? Only the one who believes that Jesus is the Son of God."

1.  Have you ever felt like the devil is trying to devour you or trying to get you to doubt your faith? How so?

2.  Do you feel the Holy Spirit's work in you? Perhaps He's helped you endure through a long trial, or perhaps you feel Him leading you to do the right thing and resist sin.

# Daily Prayer

Father in heaven, thank You that because You overcame the world, we can overcome as well. Lord, we know that the devil will do anything to try to get us to doubt our faith. We live in a society that is anti-Christian and that tries to mock us and deceive us. Help us to stand firm in the truth. Lord, we know that we are able to stand firm because Your Holy Spirit lives within us. We ask that You give us strength to endure and to discern what is right and wrong. Help us to believe that we will overcome trials and suffering because You are in us, and You are far greater than any attack from the enemy. Thank You for Your blood that was shed at the cross and for Your resurrection. You defeated death and darkness! You have overcome, and we too overcome because You have washed us clean, and because You live inside us.

# Twenty-eight

## PERSEVERANCE

Christians are told to rejoice in their sufferings. To the world, this might sound odd. Even many believers ask, "How am I supposed to rejoice in my sufferings?" Because God's Word tells us that trials lead to perseverance. James 1:2–4 (NIV) says, "Consider it pure joy, my brothers and sisters, whenever you face trials of many kinds, because you know that the testing of your faith produces perseverance. Let perseverance finish its work so that you may be mature and complete, not lacking anything." James says that trials are "the testing of our faith." When trials come our way, whatever they may be, do we get angry at God and stop trusting in Him? Or do we continue to trust Him and seek Him in the suffering? When life got hard for Job and his wife, she told Job to "curse God and die." But Job refused, and he continued to stay faithful to God. He persevered.

A true believer will continue to trust God and seek Him, no matter how difficult life's trials may get. They will not abandon their faith. This is the help of the Holy Spirit, as we talked about in the previous devotion. "The saints prove their conversion by their perseverance, and that perseverance comes from a continual supply of divine grace to their souls," said Spurgeon. This doesn't mean that true believers won't struggle or have questions when hard times come. Consider David. He asked, "Why, Lord, do you stand far off? Why do you hide yourself in times of trouble" (Psalm 10:1 NIV)? But even though he had questions, he continued to praise God and to trust in Him. He persevered. Remember how in the previous devotion we talked about the work of the Holy Spirit in our lives. It is He who gives us strength. David, Job, Joseph, Paul, and believers today are able to stand firm in their faith not by their own strength but by the power of the Holy Spirit working within them. Remember this verse which I quote often in this devotional: "He who began a good work in you will carry it on to completion" (Philippians 1:6 NIV).

James tells us that "the testing of our faith produces perseverance." When we continue to trust and seek God through the trials and the suffering, no matter how long or difficult they may be, we persevere. Why is perseverance such a good thing? James tells us that it leads to a "mature and complete believer, not lacking anything." The trials of this life help us to grow spiritually. They strengthen our faith, they humble us, they teach us lessons, and they draw us closer to the Lord. Spurgeon said, "It is quite clear from scripture that through believers' suffering, God refines them like gold in a furnace. When the gold knows why it is in the fire, it will thank the refiner and will find a sweet satisfaction even in the flames." I think of the apostle Paul who said, "We glory in our sufferings, because we know that suffering produces perseverance" (Romans 5:3 NIV). And the Lord rewards those who persevere. James 1:12 (NIV) says, "Blessed is the one who perseveres under trial because, having stood the test, that person will receive the crown of life that the Lord has promised to those who love him."

Are you going through a trial? Remember that staying faithful to Christ will produce perseverance which will lead to a more mature and complete believer. And remember that God is pleased with those who persevere. He will reward them. Not only with the crown of life but perhaps even here on earth. Consider Job. He persevered through his trial. "And the Lord gave Job twice as much as he had before" (Job 42:10 ESV). James 5:11 (NLT) says, "We give great honor to those who endure under suffering. For instance, you know about Job, a man of great endurance. You can see how the Lord was kind to him at the end, for the Lord is full of tenderness and mercy." I'm sure that Job, and all of the other believers who persevered and have gone on to be with the Lord, would tell you that the temporal sufferings of this life are *well worth* it when we persevere.

So, if you are going through a trial, continue to trust God. Continue to seek after Him. Continue to praise Him. And rejoice knowing that this will lead to perseverance. Remember that God is "full of tenderness and mercy." He cares about you, and perhaps that's why He is allowing your trial. So that you have the opportunity to persevere and to become a more mature believer. And remember the reward that awaits those who persevere. The trials of this life are hard. But they are only temporary and "are not worth comparing with the glory that is to be revealed to us" (Romans 8:18 ESV).

1. When suffering, do you have questions like the ones that David had? Do you continue to stay faithful to God, even with the questions and uncertainty?

2. Has this devotion made it easier for you to rejoice in your sufferings, knowing that they lead to perseverance?

# Daily Prayer

Father in heaven, thank You that believers are able to rejoice in their sufferings. Unlike the world, who has no hope, we know that suffering leads to perseverance and to a more mature believer. We know that You are with us in the suffering and that You are full of compassion and mercy. Help us to be like Job. Though he suffered greatly, he persevered. He did not abandon his faith in You. And Lord, just as You rewarded Job for his perseverance, Your Word tells us that we will be rewarded as well. When we are worn and discouraged from our trials, help us to remember all of these truths. Help us to continue to trust You and praise You, even if we don't understand why You're allowing our trials. And help us to remember the reward that awaits those who persevere.

# Twenty-nine

## Rejoice in Trials

In our last devotion, we talked about perseverance. God's Word tells us that we can rejoice in our sufferings because they lead to perseverance, and when we persevere, we are more mature and complete believers. Persevering through our trials also leads to reward. But perseverance isn't the only reason why we should rejoice in our trials. The Bible gives us several other reasons why we, as believers, can rejoice in trials. Romans 8:28 (NIV) says, "We know that in all things God works for the good of those who love him, who have been called according to his purpose." When we are suffering, we can rejoice knowing that God will use the suffering for our good. We may not see how anything good could come from it, but God can see the good. God sees the big picture. He sees our future, and perhaps He is using the suffering that you are going through right now to prepare you for a future that you never could have imagined.

Habakkuk was able to rejoice in his trials. He says, "Though the fig tree does not bud and there are no grapes on the vines, though the olive crop fails and the fields produce no food, though there are no sheep in the pen and no cattle in the stalls, *yet I will rejoice in the Lord,* I will be joyful in God my Savior. The Sovereign Lord is my strength; he makes my feet like the feet of a deer, he enables me to tread on the heights" (Habakkuk 3:17-19, NIV; emphasis added). Habakkuk's joy wasn't dependent on material possessions. He knew that even in the trials, God was still good. He knew that His salvation was from God, and He knew that God would never leave him. He could rejoice knowing that God was walking with him every step of the way, and that God would give him strength to endure.

Another reason why we can rejoice in our sufferings is because we have the opportunity to become more like Christ. Rather than complain about our situation, or worry about it, we should trust God and have peace knowing that He is in complete control. 1 Peter 2:23 (NIV) says, "When they hurled their insults at him, he did not retaliate; when he suffered, he made no threats. Instead, he entrusted himself to him who judges justly." When Jesus suffered, He didn't complain about it. He could have walked away from the suffering if He chose to. But He trusted His Father completely. It can be easy to complain when we suffer. I know that I have a tendency to complain. Many times, I've complained about the side effects of my medicine, not being able to drive, the doctors, or the anxiety that comes upon me. But instead, I should be like Christ and trust completely in God. He is the one who is in control, and just as He used Jesus's suffering to bring salvation to the world, He will use our suffering for good as well.

Another reason to rejoice in trials is because they help us to learn more about God and His ways. Psalm 119:71 (ESV) says, "It is good for me that I was afflicted, that I might learn your statutes." When we go through trials, we tend to seek God more. We seek Him more through prayer, through His Word, and through listening to preaching. Over the past several years, I have learned so much on things, such as anxiety, depression, assurance, God's grace, and His compassion, because I have studied Bible passages on these topics, listened to preaching, read books, etc. God has reminded me of His unfailing love, His faithfulness, and His compassion.

We can also rejoice because God often uses suffering to draw us closer to Him. Before a trial, perhaps we don't pray very often or read God's Word often because everything is going well. But when a trial comes our way, we are more likely to run to Christ for help and comfort. "In suffering then, it is not only the case that we get to draw nearer to Christ, becoming more like him and leaning more fully on him. In such times Christ draws near to us to walk with his people in the furnace. And not only to walk with us but to bear us through" (Spurgeon).

Paul gives us another reason to rejoice in suffering. When Paul was suffering, Jesus said, "My grace is sufficient for you, for my power is made perfect in weakness" (2 Corinthians 12:9 NIV). Paul said, "Therefore, I will boast all the more gladly about my weaknesses, so that Christ's power may rest on me. That is why, for Christ's sake, I delight in weaknesses, in insults, in hardships, in persecutions, in difficulties. For when I am weak, then I am strong" (2 Corinthians 12:9–10 NIV). Christ can use our sufferings and weaknesses to reveal His power and to reveal His grace.

Another reason we can rejoice is because we know that this world is not our home. This life on earth is short, and though it can be filled with suffering, we know that our eternal home will be free of suffering. We know that "what we suffer now is nothing compared to the glory he will reveal to us later" (Romans 8:18 NLT). As believers then, we have many reasons to rejoice and have peace in our trials. When the world sees us rejoicing in our trials, they may wonder why. This gives us the perfect opportunity to share Jesus and His Word with them.

1. Do you find that suffering draws you nearer to Christ? Do you seek Him more in the hard times?

2. Are you able to rejoice in your sufferings knowing the good that can come from them?

# Daily Prayer

Father in heaven, thank You that we can rejoice in our sufferings. Your Word gives us many reasons why we, as Your children, can rejoice during afflictions. Thank You that the sufferings of this life are not pointless. You use them for many reasons, whether they be to help us learn more about You, to help us become more like You, to seek You more, or to reveal Your glory. And just as You used the sufferings of many believers in the Bible for a greater good, we can trust that You will use our sufferings for good as well. Help us to rejoice in our sufferings and to have peace knowing that You are in control of our situation and our lives. Help us to seek You more and to continue to praise You and trust You no matter what we are facing.

# *Thirty*

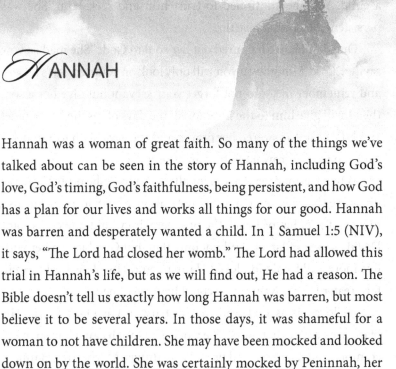

## *H*ANNAH

Hannah was a woman of great faith. So many of the things we've talked about can be seen in the story of Hannah, including God's love, God's timing, God's faithfulness, being persistent, and how God has a plan for our lives and works all things for our good. Hannah was barren and desperately wanted a child. In 1 Samuel 1:5 (NIV), it says, "The Lord had closed her womb." The Lord had allowed this trial in Hannah's life, but as we will find out, He had a reason. The Bible doesn't tell us exactly how long Hannah was barren, but most believe it to be several years. In those days, it was shameful for a woman to not have children. She may have been mocked and looked down on by the world. She was certainly mocked by Peninnah, her husband's other wife, who had several children. "Peninnah would taunt Hannah and make fun of her because the Lord had kept her from having children. Year after year it was the same—Peninnah would taunt Hannah as they went to the Tabernacle. Each time, Hannah would be reduced to tears and would not even eat" (1 Samuel 1:6–7 NLT).

To the world, Peninnah may have looked like the successful one. She was the one with several children. People may have looked down on Hannah and judged her, but remember that "people look at outward appearance, but the Lord looks at the heart" (1 Samuel 16:7 NIV). Hannah may have felt shame. She may have felt insignificant. She may have felt abandoned or unloved by God. She probably wondered why God wasn't answering her prayers and giving her a child. Yet, she continued to trust him and seek Him. She was persistent. She didn't give up.

One day, Hannah poured out her soul to God. "She made a vow saying, 'Lord Almighty, if you will only look on your servant's misery and remember me, and not forget your servant but give her a son, then I will give him to the Lord for all the days of his life'" (1 Samuel 1:11 NIV). God answered her prayer, and she gave birth to Samuel, a son who would grow up to be a great prophet.

When Hannah was barren for all those years, she probably never imagined that she would one day, not only give birth to a son, but also to a great prophet of Israel, the prophet who would one day anoint David as king of Israel. And not only that, but God blessed her with five more children! God loved Hannah, and His plans for her were far greater than anything she could have imagined.

He loves us as well, and we can trust in His plans for us. His plans are greater than ours. The story of Hannah can bring so much comfort, and it can remind us of many things. Maybe, like Hannah, you've been going through a trial for years and you've been praying, but your prayers haven't been answered. Maybe you've even been mocked or looked down on by the world for whatever you're going through. Don't give up. Continue to seek God and pour out your heart to Him. Trust in Him and His plan. Wait for God's perfect timing.

We don't know for sure why God waited so long to answer Hannah's prayers, but we have some ideas. If Samuel had been born any sooner, he may have missed the opportunity to anoint David as king. As we all know, David was a great king of Israel, and Jesus came from David's lineage. Or perhaps God was waiting until Hannah reached a point in which she was willing to give her son totally to God for His purposes. When Samuel was weaned, Hannah brought him to the tabernacle and gave him to the Lord as she had promised. He grew up in the tabernacle and was a helper of Eli, the high priest. One night, God spoke to Samuel, and from that moment on, he was a prophet of Israel.

Another reason why God may have waited to give Hannah a child was so that she could have the opportunity to persevere (which she did). And remember that God rewards persistence and perseverance. He rewarded Hannah with not only the son she prayed for, but with five more children! Hebrews 11:6 (NIV) says, "Without faith it is impossible to please God, because anyone who comes to him must believe that he exists and that he rewards those who earnestly seek him." Just as Hannah came to God in faith and continued to seek Him earnestly, we must do the same. Remember that God hears you. He cares about you. And He has a plan far greater than anything that you could imagine. Wait for His perfect timing. Psalm 27:14 (NIV) says, "Wait for the Lord; be strong, and let your heart take courage; wait for the Lord."

1.  Can you relate to Hannah in any way? Perhaps you are going through a trial in which you feel shame, or perhaps you've been praying for years but God seems silent.

2.  Have you ever, like Hannah, seen the hand of God in your life? Perhaps He delivered you from a trial after several years of praying. Perhaps He granted your request and gave you even more than you imagined.

# Daily Prayer

Father in heaven, thank You for all the things that we can learn from Hannah's story. Lord, You saw her in her distress, and You cared. You had a plan in mind for her, one that she never could have dreamed of. Lord, help us to be persistent like Hannah. Help us not to lose hope but to continue to seek You and trust in You. Help us to be patient, knowing that Your timing is perfect. Lord, help us to remember that You "reward those who diligently seek You."

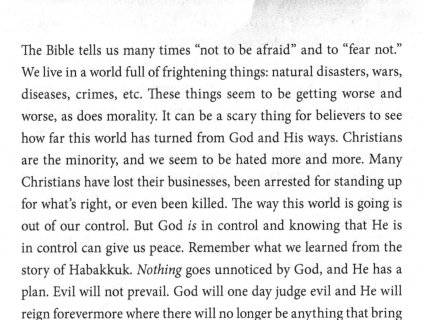

# Thirty-one

## Fear Not

The Bible tells us many times "not to be afraid" and to "fear not." We live in a world full of frightening things: natural disasters, wars, diseases, crimes, etc. These things seem to be getting worse and worse, as does morality. It can be a scary thing for believers to see how far this world has turned from God and His ways. Christians are the minority, and we seem to be hated more and more. Many Christians have lost their businesses, been arrested for standing up for what's right, or even been killed. The way this world is going is out of our control. But God *is* in control and knowing that He is in control can give us peace. Remember what we learned from the story of Habakkuk. *Nothing* goes unnoticed by God, and He has a plan. Evil will not prevail. God will one day judge evil and He will reign forevermore where there will no longer be anything that bring us fear.

When we are afraid, we must do the same thing that we do when we have anxiety. We must remind ourselves that God is always with us, we must present our fears to Him, and we must trust that He is in control. One of my favorite Bible verses is Isaiah 41:10 (ESV), which says, "Fear not, for I am with you; be not dismayed, for I am your God." It can be easy to become fearful or dismayed in these days, but

God tells us not to fear or be dismayed *because* He is with us. Because we serve the God of all creation, we need not fear. The same God that created the universe is with you and me. That's an amazing thing to think about! Sometimes when I am afraid, I will just quote that verse over and over again in my head. God is not only with us, but He also promises to *never* leave us. "Never will I leave you; never will I forsake you" (Hebrews 13:5 NIV). When we are afraid, it can feel like God is far away, but He hasn't left your side. He promised to never leave you. Reminding yourself of this truth can bring great comfort.

In Psalm 23:4 (ESV), David wrote, "Even though I walk through the valley of the shadow of death, I will fear no evil, for you are with me; your rod and your staff, they comfort me." Maybe you are walking through a dark valley, and it has brought you fear. Remember who is with you. Remember to turn your eyes to Him, and He will give you comfort. We can rest knowing that our Good Shepherd is greater than anything that brings us fear. He was stronger than the lions that Daniel faced, stronger than the burning furnace that Shadrach, Meshach, and Abednego faced, stronger than Goliath, stronger than Pharaoh and his armies, stronger than any sickness, and stronger than sin and death. He is stronger than the things in today's world that bring us fear.

Present your fears to Him, whatever they may be. And then trust that He is in control. Rest in the arms of the Good Shepherd and let Him fight the battle. He has the power to take away whatever it is that's bringing you fear, but even if He doesn't, we can rest in His arms knowing that whatever happens is what's best for us. "As the heavens are higher than the earth, so are my ways higher than your ways and my thoughts than your thoughts" (Isaiah 55:9 NIV).

Jesus is calling us to take our eyes off ourselves and our fears and to put them onto Him. So often we forget that Jesus is right here with us, that He cares about us, and that we can trust Him. We look at the wind and waves (our fears) rather than at Christ. In Psalm 46 (NIV), the psalmist imagines some of the most fearful events that could occur, but he knows that God is greater than all of them. He knows that he can rest knowing God is always with him, and that God is in control. The passage says, "God is our refuge and strength, an ever-present help in trouble. Therefore we will not fear, though the earth give way and the mountains fall into the heart of the sea, though its waters roar and foam and the mountains quake with their surging … He says, "Be still, and know that I am God." When circumstances try to fill you with fear, remember to be still and know that God is on the throne. He is in control. Turn your eyes to Jesus. Trust that He is with you. Trust that He loves you. Trust that He has the power to defeat whatever is bringing you fear, but even if He doesn't, He has a good reason why. He has a plan for your life.

1.   What are some things that try to bring you fear?


2.   What do you do when fear arises?

# Daily Prayer

Father in heaven, thank You that we do not need to fear. Many times in Your Word You tell us to "fear not." We live in a world that is full of frightening things. It can be easy to become filled with fear. As believers though, we do not need to fear. We know that nothing goes unnoticed by You. We know that You are our Good Shepherd. You are so much stronger than anything that we may face. Lord, the next time that we are afraid, help us to remember that You are with us and that You never leave us. Help us to give our fears to You and to trust that You are in control. Help us to trust that whatever happens is what's best for us. Help us to rest in Your arms, knowing that You love us, and You take good care of us.

# Thirty-two

## JESUS GIVES US REST

"Come to me, all you who are weary and burdened, and I will give you rest. Take my yoke upon you and learn from me, for I am gentle and humble in heart, and you will find rest for your souls. For my yoke is easy and my burden is light" (Matthew 11:28–30 NIV). At the time that Jesus preached this, the Pharisees were laying heavy burdens on the shoulders of the people. The Pharisees were a very legalistic group who believed that one could only be saved by obeying God's law. But they also added *several* laws. This was a *huge* burden to the Jews as no one could obey all of these laws.

Jesus called the Pharisees hypocrites. He said, "They preach, but do not practice. They tie up heavy burdens, hard to bear, and lay them on people's shoulders, but they themselves are not willing to move them with their finger. They do all their deeds to be seen by others" (Matthew 23:3–5 ESV). The Pharisees made people believe that works were the only way to be saved, and they tried to turn the people away from Christ. They were prideful and wanted others to see how "good" they were. But they missed the whole point of the gospel. They failed to humble themselves and admit that they could never be good enough. They failed to see that they desperately needed Jesus and His grace. Unlike Jesus, who said that He is "gentle and humble," the Pharisees were harsh toward the people, and they were proud of their status. They thought highly of themselves and looked down on others. As Christians, we know that we could never be saved by our works. We know that "all have sinned and fall short of the glory of God" (Romans 3:23 NIV). We could never be good enough. But we know that Jesus *is* good enough. And it is Jesus who makes us clean. If you've put your faith in Jesus, then you are cleansed and forgiven!

But sometimes, even believers can fall into the "Pharisee trap." Sometimes, we forget that we are simply saved by God's grace. We don't have to "be good enough." That is why Jesus told the Jewish people to come to Him and find rest. We can rest knowing that Jesus, and what He's done, has saved us—not our works. Or perhaps sometimes we even become prideful and look down on nonbelievers, thinking that we are better. But we needed God's grace just as desperately as they do, and God is calling them to come to Him and find rest as well. I know that I've fallen into the "Pharisee trap." I've mentioned that I struggle with scrupulosity (a religious OCD). Many times, I look at myself and the things that I'm doing rather than to Christ and what He's done for me. I'll look at myself and ask questions, such as *Do I have all the fruits of the spirit? What if my faith isn't strong enough? Am I serving enough?* I fall into a legalistic state of mind rather than trusting in God's grace alone.

This battle in my mind can be exhausting. Just as the Pharisees made the Jews believe that they had to "be good enough" by their righteous acts (and this was exhausting to them), so also will my OCD try to convince me that I must "be good enough." But Jesus told the exhausted Jews to come to Him and find rest. When my OCD begins to flare, I must remind myself of the truth that I can rest because of Jesus and what He's done for me. I think about the thief on the cross. I can only imagine how the Pharisees must have looked down on Him and believed themselves to be so much better. But this criminal came to Jesus in his final minutes. He believed in Christ, and Jesus saved him. To God, this criminal was made as white as snow, while the Pharisees and their "righteous deeds" were like "filthy rags" in God's sight.

Do you ever believe yourself to be so much better than someone else? Remember that we are *all* sinners and that everyone needs the blood of Christ to be cleansed. Rather than looking down on the unsaved, we should remember how Christ has saved us, and we should tell them that He wants to save them as well. How much easier it is, like Jesus said, to come to Him than to try to "be good enough." All we need to do is believe in Him and receive His gift of grace. "We are justified *freely* by his grace through the redemption that came by Christ Jesus" (Romans 3:24 NIV; emphasis added).

Maybe there are times when the enemy lies to you. Maybe the enemy tells you that you aren't doing enough good works. Maybe, like the Pharisees, you are prideful and think of yourself as better than unbelievers. Remind yourself that you didn't deserve God's grace or earn it. Remind yourself that you were in desperate need of God's grace just as much as they are. If the enemy tries to deceive you by making you ask yourself if you are "good enough," remember how Jesus rejected the Pharisees. Remember how He called people to come to Him and find rest. Not only "good people." He invited *everyone.* He saved the criminal on the cross because the criminal came to Jesus. Don't look at yourself and the things that you do. Instead, look at Jesus and what He's done for you. "My faith rests *not in what I am*, or shall be, or feel, or know, *but in what Christ is,* in what He has done, and in what He is doing for me," said Spurgeon (emphasis added).

1. Do you ever fall into the "Pharisee trap" in any way? Maybe sometimes you believe that grace alone isn't enough, that you also need works. Or maybe you become prideful of your good works and look down on others.


2. Do you have to remind yourself frequently that you can rest because you've come to Jesus?

# Daily Prayer

Father in heaven, thank You for this beautiful promise that all can come to You and find rest for their souls. We don't have to worry about "being good enough." You've made us righteous by Your precious blood. When thoughts and doubts fill our minds as to whether or not we are doing enough good works, help us to reject those thoughts and to remember that we are Your children because of what *You* did and because of who *You* are, not because of what we've done or because we deserve it. Thank You for Your amazing love and amazing grace! Lord, I pray that good works would flow from us, not because we feel like we must do them but because we *want* to do them. Help us not to be prideful of our status as Christians. We needed Your grace just as desperately as the lost need Your grace. Help us to be compassionate and to have a desire to share the wonderful news about You and Your grace.

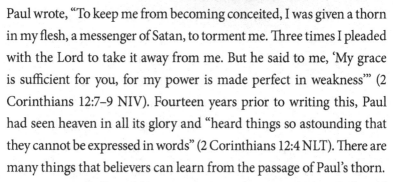

# Thirty-three

## Paul's Thorn

Paul wrote, "To keep me from becoming conceited, I was given a thorn in my flesh, a messenger of Satan, to torment me. Three times I pleaded with the Lord to take it away from me. But he said to me, 'My grace is sufficient for you, for my power is made perfect in weakness'" (2 Corinthians 12:7–9 NIV). Fourteen years prior to writing this, Paul had seen heaven in all its glory and "heard things so astounding that they cannot be expressed in words" (2 Corinthians 12:4 NLT). There are many things that believers can learn from the passage of Paul's thorn.

Just as God allowed Satan to torment Job, we see that God allowed Satan to torment Paul as well. We know that God doesn't allow suffering for no reason. Rather, He uses it for our good. We know that God loves us and that He is full of compassion. This passage tells us *why* God allowed Paul's suffering: to keep him humble. If a person saw heaven or saw the Lord Jesus Christ face-to-face, it could be very easy to become prideful. But remember that "God opposes the proud, but shows favor to the humble" (James 4:6; ESV). Perhaps God didn't want Paul going around bragging about his experience, but rather, he wanted Paul to continue sharing the gospel message.

When we ask God to deliver us from something, sometimes God says no as he did to Paul. But just as He had a reason for allowing

Paul to suffer, He has a reason for allowing our trials as well. Perhaps, like with Paul, God's reason is to keep us humble. Perhaps God's reason is to help us rely more on Him and His power. At another point in Paul's life, Paul said, "we were so utterly burdened beyond our strength that we despaired of life itself (2 cor. 1:8 ESV). But he goes on to tell the Corinthians why this happened. *But that was to make us rely not on ourselves, but on God who raises the dead* (2 Corinthians 1:9 ESV; emphasis added). When we are suffering and at our weakest, God wants us to lean on Him and trust in Him. There may be nothing that we can do to help our situation, but God is able, and He will help us to endure in our faith.

When God said no to Paul's request for deliverance from the thorn, God said, "My grace is sufficient for you" (2 Corinthians 12:9 NIV). God's grace was enough for Paul, even in Paul's weakness. Perhaps Paul believed that his thorn was keeping him from being the best person that he could be. Perhaps he feared that the Lord's grace might leave him. I know that my problems can do the same to me. I'm unable to drive, and I struggle with anxiety, depression, and side effects of medicine. I often don't feel like I'm the best person that I can be. But as we saw in the previous devotion, we don't have to be "good enough" to earn God's grace *or* to keep it. Our weaknesses don't take away God's grace or love. Rather, they show us how amazing God's grace and love are. They show us how much we need His grace and that His grace is greater than anything we face.

Jesus also told Paul that "His power is made perfect in weakness." Our weaknesses can be used by God to reveal His mighty power. We can see many other men and women in the Bible where God's power was revealed through their weakness. Think about all of the sick, blind, and lame people in the Bible. It was a weakness of theirs, but God revealed His mighty power by healing them. I think of the blind man. Jesus's disciples asked why the man was born blind. Jesus said, "This happened *so the power of God could be seen in him*" (John 9:3 NLT; emphasis added).

Or perhaps God uses our weaknesses to reveal His power in less obvious ways. As I mentioned, our weaknesses reveal how great God's grace is. We don't have to be perfect to receive God's grace. His grace can reach as far as the worst sinner. And His grace sustains the believer in their weaknesses. Perhaps He uses our weaknesses to sanctify us or to help us persevere. Whether God reveals His power in mighty ways or in less obvious ways, His "power is made perfect in weakness."

If you are going through a trial and feel like your weakness is keeping you from being the best version of yourself, remember that God's grace is still enough for you. Trust that He has a reason for saying no to your healing so far. Remember Genesis 50:20 (NIV) which says, "You intended to harm me, but God intended it for good." Satan meant to torment Paul, but God intended to keep Paul humble. And remember that God's power is made perfect in your weakness, whether it is to keep you humble and show His amazing grace, to draw you closer to Him, or to reveal His glory in a mighty way by showing you a miracle. We can have peace in any trial knowing that God has a purpose and knowing that His grace never runs out. And we can trust that His ways are always best and that "His power is made perfect in our weaknesses."

1. Do your trials and weaknesses ever make you feel like you are not able to be the best version of yourself? Do you feel like you must be strong or "good enough" in order to obtain God's grace?

2. Do you believe that God's power is made perfect in your weakness?

# Daily Prayer

Father in heaven, thank You for putting this passage in Your Word. I know that it has brought comfort to many believers, and it teaches us so many things. It teaches us that sometimes You do say no to believers' prayers. It teaches us that You do allow trials. But it also teaches us that You have a reason for the trials. It teaches us that Your grace never runs out. We don't have to be "good enough" to obtain Your grace and love. Your grace and love are all we need. And Lord, we know that Your power is made perfect in our weakness. Whatever the reason may be for You allowing our trials, it reveals Your power—whether Your reason is to keep us humble, to help us rely more on You, or to show us a miracle by delivering us from our trials. When we are suffering, help us to remember these truths. Help us to know that our suffering is not without reason. Your grace and love have not left us, and You will use our weaknesses for our good and to reveal Your power.

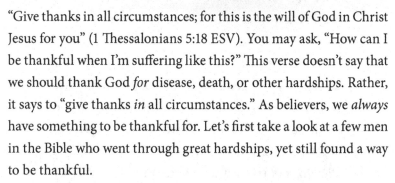

# Thirty-four

## Being Thankful

"Give thanks in all circumstances; for this is the will of God in Christ Jesus for you" (1 Thessalonians 5:18 ESV). You may ask, "How can I be thankful when I'm suffering like this?" This verse doesn't say that we should thank God *for* disease, death, or other hardships. Rather, it says to "give thanks *in* all circumstances." As believers, we *always* have something to be thankful for. Let's first take a look at a few men in the Bible who went through great hardships, yet still found a way to be thankful.

Let's first talk about Daniel. An issue had just been decreed that everyone must pray to and worship the king of Babylon. If anyone was caught praying to anyone else, they would be thrown into the lions' den. "Now when Daniel learned that the decree had been published, he went home to his upstairs room where the windows opened toward Jerusalem. Three times a day he got down on his knees and prayed, *giving thanks to his God, just as he had done before*" (Daniel 6:10 NIV; emphasis added). What do you suppose Daniel was thankful for? I'm sure that he wasn't praying, "Thank You God for this decree that has been issued." But perhaps he was thankful that God is in control of everything. Perhaps he was thankful because he knew that even if he did get caught praying and thrown into the lions' den, he could trust that God would be with him and that whatever happened was for the best. Perhaps he was thankful that he knew the one true God and that he could have a relationship with him. Perhaps he was thanking God for his salvation. We don't know what he was thanking God for, but whatever it was, he still found a way to be thankful in a difficult situation.

Then there's David. Psalm 69 tells us of David's distress because of the vast armies that were seeking to destroy him. But in the very same chapter, David wrote, "I will praise the name of God with song; I will magnify him *with thanksgiving*" (Psalm 69:30 ESV; emphasis added). Do you think that David was thanking God for the distress? Do you think he was thanking God that vast armies were seeking to destroy him? Perhaps David was thanking God for His power and all that He had done in David's life. God had anointed David, who was only a shepherd boy, to be the king of Israel. God used David to slay the giant. David knew that God had the power to rescue him from the enemies, but he also knew that even if God didn't rescue him, he could still trust God. Perhaps he was thankful for God's faithfulness to him. Perhaps he was thankful for God's love and salvation.

We also read about Jonah, who was thankful in his suffering. After being swallowed by a great fish, he still found a way to be thankful. He wrote, "I will sacrifice unto thee with the voice of *thanksgiving*" (Jonah 2:9 KJV; emphasis added). Jonah had just disobeyed God and tried to run away from Him. Perhaps Jonah was thankful that God forgives. Perhaps he was thankful that God saved him from drowning by way of the great fish. Perhaps Jonah believed that he was going to die in the fish, but he was thankful that he would go to heaven when he died.

These men of God faced great trials, but they were still able to give thanks to God. We can, and should, do the same. No matter what our trials may be, God wants us to give thanks. For believers who are diagnosed with a disease, lose a job, lose a loved one to death, or face other challenges, God wants them to be thankful. They don't have to thank God for the suffering, but they can be thankful that God has a purpose for suffering, and that He uses it for good. They can be thankful that God loves them and has compassion on them. They can be thankful that God never leaves them. They can be thankful for Christ's atoning work on the cross. They can be thankful that they have an eternity in paradise to look forward to, and the list could go on. In order to be thankful in trials, we must keep our eyes on Jesus, not on the problems that we are facing. "We fix our eyes not on what is seen, but on what is unseen, since what is seen is temporary, but what is unseen is eternal" (2 Corinthians 4:18 NIV). The problems we face in this world are temporary, but we can be thankful that we serve a God who uses our problems for good, who loves us, and who has given us an eternal home where there will be no more pain or sorrow.

1. Do you find it difficult to be thankful in hard times?

2. What are some things that you can thank God for despite the suffering you may be facing?

# Daily Prayer

Father in heaven, we have so much to be thankful for, even when we are suffering. When we are going through hard times, help us to take our eyes off our problems and to turn them to You. Help us to remember all of the things that we have to be thankful for. You have saved us from our sins. You call us Your children. We can run to You in times of trouble and know that You care. You work all things for our good. You never leave us. You are preparing a place for us where there will be no more pain or sorrow. And the list could go on. Help us to be able to give thanks to You in *all* circumstances because this is Your will. Help us to keep our eyes on what is unseen, not on what is seen.

# Thirty-five

# THE STRUGGLE WITH SIN

Are you struggling with sin? Maybe you are jealous of a person's looks or popularity. Maybe you are prideful because of your promotion or because of your status. Maybe you struggle with anger or bitterness toward a person who hurt you. For a believer, the battle with sin can become discouraging. We know that we shouldn't be sinning, and we try not to, but sometimes it just feels like a battle that we cannot win. You want to do good, but perhaps you can't carry it out completely. You want to love God with all of your heart, soul, mind, and strength, and although you love Him, perhaps you feel like you don't love him as much as you should. You want to love your neighbor as you love yourself, but no matter how hard you try, you feel like you struggle with selfishness. You want to be generous, but perhaps you feel like you just can't do it with the right attitude. You want to trust God completely, but there are many times when your faith feels weak, or you have your doubts.

Struggling with sin and struggling to do good is a battle in every believer's life. It was a battle for even the great apostle Paul. In Romans 7:18–25 (NIV), Paul wrote, "I have the desire to do what is good, but I cannot carry it out. For I do not do the good I want to do, but the evil I do not want to do- this I keep on doing. Now if I do what I do not want to do, it is no longer I who do it, but it is sin living in me that does it. So I find this law at work: Although I want to do good, evil is right there with me. For in my inner being I delight in God's law; but I see another law at work in me, waging war against the law of my mind and making me a prisoner of the law of sin at work within me. What a wretched man I am! Who will rescue me from this body that is subject to death? Thanks be to God, who delivers me through Jesus Christ our Lord! So then, I myself in my mind am a slave to God's law, but in my sinful nature a slave to the law of sin." In these verses, Paul is describing the battle between the flesh and the spirit.

Every believer has the Spirit of God living in them. The Spirit is what gives us the desire to do good. But until we receive our new, immortal bodies, our flesh will still struggle with sin. In 1 Corinthians 15:53 (KJV), Paul wrote, "This corruptible must put on incorruption, and this mortal must put on immortality." I can often feel the battle between the flesh and the Spirit. Sometimes, when my husband and I are watching a movie, I'll feel the Spirit convicting me that I shouldn't be watching that movie. While the flesh on the other hand says, "it's not that bad of a movie." The flesh wants to watch the movie. Galatians (ESV) 5:17 says, "For the desires of the flesh are against the Spirit, and the desires of the Spirit are against the flesh." Many times, I fail, and I continue to watch the movie. But other times, I listen to the voice of the Spirit, and I stop watching it. I have the desire to do what is right. I don't want to continue watching the movie if God doesn't want me to. But many times I fail. Praise God that through Jesus Christ we are delivered from these corrupted bodies.

Now this passage that Paul wrote doesn't mean that Paul never did good and that he always sinned. We know that Paul was a great apostle who went around sharing the gospel and that he was severely persecuted for his faith. It was the Spirit who led him to do that. But Paul knew that he still sinned and that he was far from being perfect. In our battle with sin, the devil likes to whisper lies into our ears, such as *Maybe God's grace will run out, Maybe God is angry at me, or Maybe I'm not really saved.* He likes us to keep our eyes on ourselves and our failures and our inability to be good enough. And we *aren't* good enough, but praise God, we have a Savior who *is* good enough!

I love how the very next chapter of Romans starts out with this verse: "Therefore, there is now no condemnation for those who are in Christ Jesus" (Romans 8:1 NIV). Maybe in your struggle with sin, you feel condemned. Maybe you don't feel like God's child. Before Christ saved us, we were condemned. But we are no longer condemned because Christ has redeemed us from our sinful flesh and has given us His Spirit. We still fail and fall short of perfection because we still live in these mortal bodies, but Christ has paid the price of all of our sins and has imputed His righteousness to us. And we look forward to the day when we will put off these old bodies and put on new bodies which no longer struggle with sin. I love this quote from John Piper: "Take heart if your soul feels like a battlefield at times. The sign of whether you are indwelt by the Spirit is not that you have no bad desires, but that you are at war with them!"

1. In what ways do you struggle with sin? Can you feel the battle between the flesh and the spirit? The flesh pulls you one way while the Spirit pulls you another.

2. What are some ways in which you desire to do good but feel like you can't carry it out completely?

# Daily Prayer

Father in heaven, thank You so much for putting these verses into Your Word. All believers experience the battle between the Spirit and the flesh. There are things we want to do, but feel like we can't, and then there are things we don't want to do, but we do anyway. This can become very discouraging. But what a comfort to know that even Paul faced the same challenge, and as Paul wrote, we know that You have redeemed us from sin, and we are not condemned. We look forward to the day when we will put off these bodies for glorious bodies, and we will no longer struggle with sin. Help us in our battle to strive to do what is good and to resist the temptations to do wrong.

# Thirty-six

## Humble Yourselves

1 Peter 5:6 (NIV) says, "Humble yourselves, therefore, under God's mighty hand, that he may lift you up in due time." Why does it say, "Humble yourselves, *therefore*"? The previous verse tells us that "God opposes the proud but shows favor to the humble." 2 Timothy 3:2 (NIV) says that in the last days people will be proud. We can certainly see that in today's society. We live in a society that encourages pride. This generation has abandoned God's Word and His commandments and instead has chosen to do as they see fit; if they think something is right, then it's right. If it makes them happy, then that's all that matters. It's all about *me* and what makes *me* happy. There is even a month called "pride month" for the LGBTQ+ community. Not only have these people chosen to sin against God in order to please themselves, but they do it with pride. If a woman says she needs her husband to lead her family, or if a person says they need God, society sees this as a weakness. People don't think they need anyone but themselves, and they believe that they have the ability to achieve anything on their own.

How do we remain humble in the midst of a prideful society? We keep our focus on God and His Word, not on the world we live in. We choose to do what the Lord says is right, not what we think is right. We strive to please the Lord, not ourselves. We recognize our dependence on the Lord and what He's done for us. We admit our failures and weaknesses and we ask the Lord for forgiveness and for strength. We don't think of ourselves as better than others. Rather than being selfish, we serve others. Philippians 2:3-4 (NIV) says, "Do nothing from selfish ambition or conceit, but in humility count others more significant than yourselves. Let each of you look not only to his own interests, but also to the interests of others."

Humility is in no way a weakness. C.S. Lewis said, "Humility is not thinking less of yourself, but thinking of yourself less." As believers, being humble doesn't mean putting ourselves down or being insecure. It's OK to be confident in who you are. And we ought to have great confidence because we have been saved from our sins, and we know where we are going! But a believer shouldn't only think about themselves and their own needs and desires. We shouldn't think of ourselves as better than others. Rather, we are to think about how we can serve the needs of others. We recognize that we are sinners and just like everyone else, we need God's grace. We should have compassion on the lost and have a desire to share the gospel with them.

I think about earlier devotions where we talked about Jehoshaphat and the Pharisees. Jehoshaphat humbled himself. He admitted that he didn't know what to do and that He needed God's help. And God showed him favor. And then there were the Pharisees who were a very proud group. They thought highly of themselves and looked down on others. They didn't think they needed anyone but themselves to earn salvation. They failed to humble themselves and admit that they needed Jesus. Jesus opposed them. But for the people who humbled themselves and said, *I need you, Lord. I could never be good enough on my own,* God showed them mercy and grace. Luke

14:11 (ESV) says, "For everyone who exalts himself will be humbled, and he who humbles himself will be exalted."

I believe Jesus is our perfect example of humility. No one is humble all the time. There are always moments when we fail and become prideful. But Jesus was always humble. Even though He is God, Creator of the universe, He was not prideful. "Jesus made himself nothing by taking the very nature of a servant, being made in human likeness ... He *humbled* himself by becoming obedient to death—even death on a cross" (Philippians 2:7–8 NIV; emphasis added)! Although Jesus is God, He stepped down from His throne for our sakes. He lived a life of obedience and serving others. He took our sins upon Himself so that we could be saved. He was totally selfless, not thinking of Himself but of others.

1 Peter 2:23 (NIV) says, "When they hurled their insults at him, he did not retaliate; when he suffered, he made no threats. Instead, he entrusted himself to him who judges justly." In our own sufferings, it can be hard not to complain. It can be hard to trust God. It can be hard to care only about what *we* want, rather than what God wants. But let us choose to be like Jesus. Let us entrust ourselves to God. This shows humility. We realize that there might be nothing that we can do to help ourselves, but we trust that God is able. And rather than trying to control the situation on our own, we are going to give it to God. And rather than caring only about ourselves and what we want, we are going to care about what God wants for us.

1. Do you sometimes find it hard to be humble? What are some things that keep you from being humble?

2. Does the society we live in ever cause you to focus more on yourself and what makes you happy?

# Daily Prayer

Father in heaven, Your Word teaches us much about humility. You desire for us to be humble. It can be very difficult to stay humble when we live in a society that encourages pride. Please help us not to be like the world. But instead, help us to keep our focus on You and Your Word. Help us to ask You for humility. Help us to strive to be like You, Jesus. Being the Creator of all the universe, You could be prideful. But instead, you showed humility by stepping down from your throne, and enduring the cross for our sakes. You entrusted Yourself to the Father. Help us to do the same when we are suffering. Help us not to complain about our suffering or to think only of ourselves. Rather, help us to give our battles to you, and help us to care about *Your* plans. Help us to be able to rejoice in our trials knowing that You are in control of our situation and You will use it for good.

# Thirty-seven

## Focus on Eternity

As children of God, we have an amazing eternal home waiting for us. Every wrong will be made right. There will be no more evil, no more sorrow, no more sickness, and no more death. We will be reunited with believers who have gone on before us. But I think the best part is that we will be with Jesus, our Lord and Savior, forevermore! Revelation 21:3-4 (ESV) says, "Behold, the dwelling place of God is with man. He will dwell with them, and they will be his people and God himself will be with them as their God. He will wipe away every tear from their eyes, and death shall be no more, neither shall there be mourning, nor crying, nor pain anymore, for the former things have passed away." Psalm 16:11 (ESV) says, "In your presence there is fullness of joy: at your right hand are pleasures forevermore."

Knowing what awaits us for all eternity should bring us great joy and hope. This world is not our home. We are only pilgrims passing through. This life on earth is so very short compared to all of eternity. Yet far too many believers are so focused on this present life that they lose sight of what lies ahead. Their main focus is on gaining earthly, material possessions: more money, better homes, better cars, better vacations, etc. They store up all these treasures on earth while forgetting to store up their treasures in heaven. Jesus said, "Do not lay up for yourselves treasures on earth, where moth and rust destroy and where thieves break in and steal. But lay up for yourselves treasures in heaven, where neither moth nor rust destroys, and where thieves do not break in and steal" (Matthew 6:19–20 ESV). Jesus said this in His famous Sermon on the Mount. In the very same sermon, He shows us a few ways in which we can store up treasures in heaven. Jesus talks about being humble. Remember in our former devotion we talked about how God hates pride but shows favor to the humble. Jesus also talked about being merciful, not worrying, trusting God, praying, turning the other cheek, seeking first the kingdom of God, being faithful to our spouses, resisting anger, and more.

There is nothing wrong with being rich in this world or having many possessions. Job was a wealthy man. It becomes a problem if we start to prioritize wealth over God. Our number one priority should be God. And our devotion should be to him. Jesus said, "You cannot serve both God and money" (Matthew 6:24 NIV). It's OK to have a lot of money, but you cannot view your money as equally as important as God. You must be willing to lose all your money and possessions if that's what it takes to follow Christ.

I want to encourage you to keep your focus on eternity—the joy that it will bring and the rewards that you will receive according to how you lived your life. Paul reminded the Corinthian believers that "we fix our eyes not on what is seen, but on what is unseen, since what is seen is temporary, but what is unseen is eternal" (2 Corinthians 4:18 NIV). Are you discouraged or worn out? Don't give up. Remember the glorious eternity that lies ahead. Maybe you're fighting a disease or you're in the dark pit of depression. Don't lose hope. Remember what lies ahead. Maybe you've lost a loved one who was a believer. 1 Thessalonians 4:13–14 (NIV) says, "Brothers and sisters, we do not want you to be uninformed about those who sleep in death, so that you do not grieve like the rest of mankind, who have no hope. For we believe that Jesus died and rose again, and so we believe that God will bring with Jesus whose who have fallen asleep in him." When we keep our eyes on Jesus and the eternity that awaits us, then the problems of this world don't seem so big. "I consider that our present sufferings are not worth comparing with the glory that will be revealed in us" (Romans 8:18 NIV). So, if you're suffering or if you've become more focused on storing up earthly treasures than heavenly treasures, remember what lies ahead. "Our citizenship is in heaven. And we eagerly await a Savior from there, the Lord Jesus Christ" (Philippians 3:20 NIV).

Everyone will stand before Christ one day. When you stand before Him, your worldly wealth and possessions won't matter. What will matter are the things you did for the kingdom of God. What did you do with the talents, resources, and opportunities that God gave you? Were you a light in this dark world? Did you devote your life to God? Did you praise Him and trust in Him? I know that when I stand before Christ, I want to hear Him say, "Well done, good and faithful servant! You have been faithful with a few things; I will put you in charge of many things. Come and share your master's happiness" (Matthew 25:23 NIV). I don't want to regret the way I lived on earth. It's reward enough to hear Him say, "Well done," but the fact that He will also put us in charge of many things is amazing! The Bible also talks about a few other rewards in heaven. It speaks about five imperishable crowns that believers have the opportunity to receive: the imperishable crown, the crown of rejoicing, the crown of righteousness, the crown of glory, and the crown of life. I'm sure there are many other rewards and treasures that we can store up in heaven as well.

2 Corinthians 5:10 (NIV) says, "We must all appear before the judgment seat of Christ, so that each of us may receive what is due

us for the things done while in the body, whether good or bad." Now keep in mind our salvation is not based on our works. But there will be different levels of rewards for what we did in this life, and these rewards are eternal, not temporary. 1 Corinthians 3:11–15 (NLT) says, "No one can lay any foundation other than the one we already have- Jesus Christ. Anyone who builds on that foundation may use a variety of materials- gold, silver, jewels, wood, hay, or straw. But on the judgment day, fire will reveal what kind of work each builder has done. The fire will show if a person's work has any value. If the work survives, that builder will receive a reward. But if the work is burned up, the builder will suffer great loss. The builder will be saved, but like someone barely escaping through a wall of flames."

Anyone who accepts Jesus Christ as their Lord and Savior will be saved. But what we did in this life after we accepted Him will determine our rewards in heaven. I don't want to regret the things that I did or didn't do. This life on earth should be to serve God, not ourselves. It can be so easy to become distracted by worldly riches and possessions. It can be so easy in our society to focus only on ourselves and what we want. And it can be easy to become distracted by the worries of this life. Let us remember to keep our eyes on eternity. The riches and the worries of this world will fade, but the rewards and the glories of heaven will be everlasting!

1. Do you sometimes forget about heavenly treasures by focusing on earthly treasures instead?

2. What are some talents or opportunities that God has given you in order to serve Him and bring glory to Him?

# $\mathcal{D}$aily $\mathcal{P}$rayer

Father in heaven, thank You so much for sending Jesus to save us and to give us eternal life. We do not deserve this, but You have given this to us *plus* the opportunity to earn rewards in heaven! Lord, help us to spend this short life on earth being obedient to You and serving You. Help us to store up treasures in heaven, not on earth. We know that earthly riches aren't bad; in fact, many times they are a blessing from You. You blessed Job with a double portion of what he originally had. But they can become a problem if we put them before You, or if we seek riches more than we seek You. I pray that our number one priority would be You and living a life of serving You. Help us not to lose sight of eternity. This life on earth is so short and the riches that we possess in this life will not matter when we stand before You. What will matter is whether or not we lived a life of obedience and service to You. And help us in our suffering to remember that this life is so short, but we have an eternity of no suffering to look forward to.

# Thirty-eight

## Jonah

We've all heard of Jonah, the man who was in the belly of a fish for three days. But there is so much more to the story than this! It teaches us about God's character. Many times, our perception of God is wrong, especially when we are going through trials. But the story of Jonah reminds us that God is full of love, mercy, and compassion. He greatly desires for all men to come to him in repentance and faith so that they may be saved. It teaches us that God has plans and His plans *always* come to pass. It teaches us that God can use bad situations and make something good come from them. It also teaches us about ourselves. It reminds us that we are sinful and that we *desperately* need God's grace. It reminds us that His grace never runs out and that He never leaves us. It reminds us that we have a lot of growing to do.

The story starts off with God commanding Jonah to go to the city of Nineveh and preach against it because of their wickedness. But instead of obeying, Jonah tries to run away from God because he doesn't want to do what God asked. Have you ever felt like God was leading you to do something that you didn't want to do? We see this other times in the Bible. For example, when God commanded Moses to lead the Israelites out of Egypt, Moses begged the Lord to send someone else. If you believe that God is calling you to do something, be obedient to His calling. His ways are *always* best, His plans *will* come to pass, and He will be with you through it all, as we see in the story of Moses and as we will see in the story of Jonah.

So, Jonah boarded a ship and headed for Tarshish, which was as far away as he believed he could get. But God sent a mighty storm, and the sailors thought that they were going to perish. They cried out to their false gods for deliverance. Then they found Jonah asleep below deck. "The captain went to him and said, 'How can you sleep? Get up and call on your God'" (Jonah 1:6 NIV)! Jonah told them about the true God and that the only way the sea would be calm was if they threw him overboard. "The sailors picked Jonah up and threw him into the raging sea, and the storm stopped at once! The sailors were awestruck by the Lord's great power, and they offered him a sacrifice and vowed to serve him" (Jonah 1:15–16 NLT).

Here we see how God used a bad situation and turned it into good. Jonah's disobedience and the raging storm led to the pagan sailors turning to God and putting their faith in Him. God can take any situation and make something good come out of it. We also see how this story points to Jesus. Jesus was below deck during a great storm and the disciples cried to Him for help. But unlike Jonah, Jesus proved that He was God's Son by calming the sea Himself. And just as the sailors were amazed, so too were the disciples. And just as Jonah had to sacrifice his life for the physical saving of the sailors, Jesus had to sacrifice His life for the spiritual saving of anyone who believes in Him. Even though Jonah deserved to die because of his disobedience, we see God's mercy as God sent a huge fish to swallow Jonah. We all deserve death as well, but God shows us mercy through Jesus. Jonah spent three days and three nights in the great fish. This also points to Jesus. In Matthew 12:40 (NIV) we read, "As Jonah was 3 days and 3 nights in the belly of a huge fish, so the Son of Man will be 3 days and 3 nights in the heart of the earth."

God caused the great fish to spit Jonah on to dry land, giving him another chance, and this time Jonah headed to Nineveh where he warned them that they only had forty days until God would destroy them. "The Ninevites believed God. A fast was proclaimed, and all of them, from the greatest to the least, put on sackcloth" (Jonah 3:5 NIV). "When God saw what they did and how they turned from their evil ways, He relented and did not bring upon them the destruction he had threatened" (Jonah 3:10 NIV). Here we see the Lord's great mercy and compassion. We see that "if we confess our sins, he is faithful and just to forgive us our sins" (1 John 1:9 NIV). When Jonah saw that God did not punish them, he was actually *angry* at God. He had hoped that the Ninevites would be destroyed.

Perhaps Jonah was angry because the Ninevites were Gentiles, and Jonah believed that salvation was only for the Jews. Perhaps Jonah was angry because Ninevah deserved punishment. And they did. But Jonah failed to realize that He deserved punishment just as much as they did. You may recall in a previous devotion that God's grace can reach the worst of sinners. When the Ninevites turned to God, He gave them grace. The Ninevites were terribly wicked, yet God showed them forgiveness, mercy, and compassion. Jonah, on the other hand, had trouble showing forgiveness, mercy, and compassion.

While Jonah was outside the city, God allowed a plant to grow to provide him with shade. Here, we see Jonah happy for the first time. But as soon as the plant dies, Jonah is angry again. It appears that Jonah is very selfish, caring only about himself and not about the hundreds of thousands of people in Nineveh. It's easy to point fingers at Jonah, but we all struggle with the same things. We've all struggled with selfishness at times. We've all struggled to forgive someone who hurt us. We've all struggled to show mercy to people who don't deserve it. And we've all had times where we've struggled to feel compassion towards someone. This shows just how far from perfect we are and how much we still need to grow. It shows just how much we need God's grace.

We have been redeemed only because of what Christ has done, not because any of us deserves it. Our hearts should be as God's heart: merciful, forgiving, compassionate, and desiring to see men come to Him. But we all need God's help in these areas, and we should pray that He would help us to be more like Him. We see that even a prophet of God struggled with many of the same sins that we struggle with, and praise God, that just as God never left Jonah, He never leaves us or stops loving us. His grace didn't leave Jonah, and it doesn't leave us. God used the situation to teach Jonah, and He uses our situations as well to teach us and to grow us.

The book of Jonah certainly teaches us much about both God and ourselves. God showed mercy and compassion on Jonah, even though Jonah had sinned. But then when God showed mercy and compassion on the Ninevites, Jonah was angry. It's a reminder of the Lord's gracious character. But it's also a reminder of how sinful we are as humans, and how much we need God's grace. It's a reminder of how much growing we still have to do. Praise God for His compassion, His mercy, His grace, and His love which never fails us- even though we mess up time and time again.

1. Do you ever have the wrong perception of God? Perhaps instead of seeing Him as loving, forgiving and compassionate, you see Him differently.

2. Have you ever been like Jonah in any way? Maybe you ran from God's calling? Or maybe you failed to show forgiveness, mercy, or compassion to someone.

# Daily Prayer

Father in heaven, thank You for the story of Jonah. This story not only points to Jesus in so many ways, but it also reveals Your character. We see Your mercy and Your grace. We see Your compassion. We see how You desire all men to come to You in repentance. We see that You keep Your promises. Thank You for who You are. Lord, this story also shows us the sinfulness of men. It's easy to point fingers at Jonah, but we mess up all the time too, and we desperately need Your grace. Thank You that Your grace never runs out. Lord, help us to always remember Your character and what You've done for us. Help us to strive to be more like You.

# Thirty-nine

# Don't Let Fear Hold You Back

Many times, we let fear hold us back. Not only from doing the things *we* want to do, but also from doing the things that we believe *God* wants us to do. Fear has held me back many times. It's held me back from going out with friends, from going to the store, and even sometimes from going to church. The fear tries to tell me that I might have a seizure in front of people and that it would be embarrassing. The fear tries to tell me that I'd be safer if I just stayed at home, and that I wouldn't have to worry if I just stayed home.

Recently, I was offered a teaching position at the Christian school where my children attend. It was the longest I had gone in several years without a seizure, and I was *finally* able to drive again. I was offered to teach third grade, which is the grade I had hoped to teach. Everything was pointing to taking the position. I believed that perhaps these were signs that God wanted me to accept the position, but my fear was holding me back. I feared having a seizure in the classroom. Fear told me that it would be a lot easier to just stay home. Instead of trusting in God and trusting that He is in control, fear tries to tell us that we are in control. Instead of trusting that He will provide for our needs and take care of us, fear tries to get us to doubt this.

I think Moses is the greatest example of fear and of God's provision. The Lord wanted Moses to complete a *huge* task. He had chosen Moses to bring the Israelites out of Egypt and lead them to the Promised Land. But Moses was afraid. He said, "Who am I that I should go to Pharaoh and bring the Israelites out of Egypt? And God said, 'I will be with you'" (Exodus 3:11–12 NIV). Even after God said this, Moses still had his doubts. He said, "What if they do not believe me or listen to me and say, 'the Lord did not appear to you'" (Exodus 4:1 NIV)? The Lord gave Moses signs that he could show the people to prove that God had sent him. Moses was *still* hesitant and said, "Pardon your servant, Lord. I have never been eloquent, neither in the past, nor since you have spoken to your servant. I am slow of speech and tongue" (Exodus 4:10 NIV). God said, "I will help you speak and will teach you what to say" (Exodus 4:12 NIV).

Even after all of the assurance the Lord had given him, Moses was *still* afraid and full of doubts. He begged the Lord to send someone else. His fear was holding him back from doing what God wanted him to do. His fear led him to believe that he was in control rather than God. His fear filled him with doubts. But eventually, Moses did complete the task the Lord had called him to do, and God was with him every step of the way. God fulfilled his promises to Moses, and it was only by the guidance and power of God that Moses was able to fulfill God's calling in his life. It wasn't by the strength of Moses that the Israelites were freed but by the hand of God, who used Moses to fulfill His purposes. God used Moses, a fearful man who was not an eloquent speaker, to do a great thing. "God chose weak things of the world to shame the strong" (1 Corinthians 1:27 NIV).

This story is an encouragement to me. I often feel like Moses. I believed God was calling me to teach, and I kept saying, *But God,*

*I have epilepsy. God, what if I have a seizure in the classroom. God, please choose someone else.* But just as God called Moses to a task and He provided for him, God will do the same for us as well when He calls us to a task. His plans will surely come to pass.

I also think about the story of Gideon. Gideon, just an ordinary man, was asked to take an Israelite army and defeat the Midianites. Gideon was fearful, and he doubted his ability to fulfill God's task. He failed to realize that it wouldn't be by his own strength that the Israelites would be freed but by God's strength. He wanted reassurance from God, just as Moses did, and he asked God to give him *clear* signs. Finally, Gideon obeyed God's calling, and the Midianites were defeated, just as God had said.

I believed that God was calling me to take the teaching position, but just as Gideon wanted more signs—clear signs, I wanted more as well. I wanted to hear an audible voice from God saying, "Kelly, I want you to teach." Sometimes, God does give us a clear sign. But sometimes, He just wants us to seek Him for wisdom and guidance. He wants us to humbly say, "Your will be done," and then do what we believe is the right thing to do.

God didn't give me a clear sign initially, so I accepted the job because I believed this was the right decision, but I never had peace about my decision. Well, a couple of days after accepting the position, I had a seizure. I was very disappointed because I thought that perhaps I had been healed. I was so excited that I could *finally* drive again. The fact that I had gone over three months seizure free and was able to drive were some of the reasons I believed God was calling me to teach. I emailed the principal of the school, telling her about my seizure and that I'd try my best, but that I may not be very reliable because I wouldn't be able to drive. She responded that now must not be God's timing. I believe this was the clear sign that I had been asking for, and I had great peace.

I believe God was testing me. He wanted to see if I would step out in faith and obey Him, even if the task was fearful. Isaiah 41:10 (ESV) says, "Fear not, for I am with you; be not dismayed, for I am your God; I will strengthen you, I will help you." I think of Abraham. God asked him to sacrifice his son. God did this to test Abraham. To see if Abraham would be willing to do *anything* that God asked him to do. Abraham was willing, but when the time came for Abraham to sacrifice Isaac, God told him not to.

If God is calling you to a fearful task, you can trust that He is with you every step of the way, and that He will give you the strength and the help that you need to fulfill His purposes, just as He did for Moses and Gideon. If you aren't sure whether or not God is calling you to a task, continue to pray that God would help you to make the right decision. Pray that His will be done, not yours. He will surely lead you in the right direction. This life on earth shouldn't be a life of fear but of serving and trusting God. We must trust that God will use us, and that He will help us. But how can we be used if we refuse to obey Him because our fear is holding us back? There is always reward in obedience. Even if the journey God wants us to take is frightening and difficult, it will lead to great reward if we obey Him and trust Him to carry us through.

1. Have you ever believed that God was calling you to a fearful task? What was your response?

2. Do you tend to let fear hold you back from doing the things that you believe God would have you to do?

# Daily Prayer

Father in heaven, thank You that we do not have to live in fear. Sometimes You call us to do things that are fearful. If we believe that You are calling us to do something, help us to step out in faith. Help us to trust that You will be with us and that You will provide for us. Help us to trust that You reward obedience. Lord, sometimes it is difficult to know whether You are calling us to do something or not. And just as Gideon wanted clear signs that You were calling him to go up against the Midianites, we often want clear signs as well, signs that assure us that You want us to do this or that. Even if we do not get a clear sign, help us to pray that Your will would be done, and then help us to do what we believe You would have us do. Help us to trust that You will lead us to make the right choice.

# Forty

## Those Verses We Question

If you're anything like me, there are several verses that have brought questions to your mind, such as Mark 11:24 (NIV), which says, "Therefore I tell you, whatever you ask in prayer, believe that you have received it, and it will be yours." Matthew 21:22 (NIV) says, "And whatever you ask in prayer, you will receive, if you have faith." Verses like these used to bother me. I would think, *Maybe I don't have enough faith and that's why I haven't been healed.* The devil would try to use these kinds of thoughts to devour me, but God has comforted me and shown me the truth. I was so focused on these two verses, that I didn't think about the many other verses which speak on prayer.

If I ask God for a billion dollars and believe that I have received it, does that mean that a billion dollars will show up in my bank account? Or if I ask God for it to be summer all year long, does that mean that there will be no other seasons?

We will only receive what we ask of God if it is according to His will. 1 John 5:14 (NIV; emphasis added) says, "If we ask anything *according to his will*, he hears us." And we can be certain that His will for us is what's best. God only wants what's best for His children, just as we want what is best for our children. In Matthew 7:11 (NIV), Jesus says, "If you, then, though you are evil, know how to give good gifts to your children, how much more will your Father in heaven give good gifts to those who ask him!" If our children ask for a bowl of sugar for dinner, we are going to say no. Not because we want to be mean but because we care about them and want what is best for them. Likewise, if we ask for healing, God might say no, and it isn't because He doesn't care. We've talked about how God is full of compassion. He says no because healing isn't what would be best. We may not understand why, but this is where we learn to trust him and lean not on our own understanding.

In Matthew 6, Jesus is teaching His disciples how to pray. In verse 10 (NIV; emphasis added), He says, "your kingdom come, *your will be done,* on earth as it is in heaven." Notice in Luke 22:42–43 (NIV; emphasis added) Jesus is praying, and He doesn't pray for His will to be done but for the Father's will to be done. Jesus knows the great suffering that is about to come upon Him, and He asks the Father if there is any other way. He says, "Father, if *you are willing,* take this cup from me; *yet not my will, but yours be done.* An angel from heaven appeared to Him and strengthened Him." If people received everything that they asked for in prayer, then the cup would have been taken from Jesus and He wouldn't have had to suffer. But God knew that the suffering, death, and resurrection of Jesus was the only way that humankind could be saved, and this was God's will. The Father showed His compassion by sending an angel to give Jesus strength and comfort.

When God says no to our requests, it is always because He has a greater plan in mind. And just as He had compassion and comforted Jesus, He has compassion for us as well, and He comforts us as we endure our trials.

We can see other people in the Bible who God said no to. Paul begged the Lord to take away the "thorn in his flesh" that was tormenting him. If you take verses such as Matthew 21:22 (NIV) out of context, you might think, *well, Paul had faith so he should have received his request.* It wasn't part of God's will though to remove the thorn. Not because God is mean but because God knew what was best for His child. He knew that the thorn would keep Paul humble.

James 4:3 (ESV) says, "When you ask, you do not receive, because you ask wrongly, to spend it on your passions." Oftentimes, believers only care about what *they* want. Rather than wanting God's will to be done and then trusting that His will is what's best, they want things to go the way *they* plan. I used to ask God for healing from epilepsy because *I* wanted to be able to drive, *I* didn't want to be on medicine, *I* didn't want to have to worry about having a seizure, etc. All I thought about was me and what I wanted. I thought that being healed would be best. I was unhappy, and any time I had a seizure, I would get very frustrated. I wondered why God wasn't answering my prayers. But now I understand that I only cared about what I wanted. I didn't care about what God wanted.

Now when I pray, I ask for healing, but I also ask for His will to be done. And I know that His will is what's best. I have peace and contentment now, and even joy in my trial, because I know that God's will is being done in my life. I know that His ways are best, and that He will use this trial for my good.

So, if God has said no to your requests, don't be discouraged. Remember to pray that His will be done, not yours. You can trust that His will is what's best. He loves His children enough to watch His Son suffer and die so that we could have eternal life. And just as we love our children and often say no to them because we want what's best for them, so too does God often say no to His children because He wants what's best for us.

1. Have you ever, like me, read those verses about healing and wondered if maybe you weren't being healed because you didn't have enough faith?

2. When you pray, do you only care about what you want, or do you want God's will to be done, even if it means suffering?

# *Daily Prayer*

Father in heaven, thank You for wanting what is best for Your children. Lord, just as we say no to our children many times because we know what is best for them, You also say no to us many times because You know what is best for us. Many times, we think that we know what is best, and we only care about what we want. Lord, help us to want what You want. Help us to trust that Your plans are greater than ours, and that You are working all things for our good. Help us to pray that Your will be done, not ours. Please give us peace and joy in our trials knowing that Your will is being done in our lives, and Your will is what's best for us.

Printed in the United States
by Baker & Taylor Publisher Services